Programed Ear Training   **VOLUME II: MELODY AND RHYTHM**

Programed Ear Training
Volume II: MELODY AND RHYTHM

Leo Horacek and Gerald Lefkoff
West Virginia University

Under the General Editorship of
Guy Alan Bockmon
University of Tennessee

HARCOURT, BRACE & WORLD, INC.

New York   Chicago   San Francisco   Atlanta

ISBN: 0-15-572016-3
Library of Congress Catalog Number: 70-110129

Printed in the United States of America

Preface to the Instructor

PROGRAMED EAR TRAINING is designed to develop the hearing and notational skills required in the freshman and sophomore music theory courses. It consists of four programed workbooks and accompanying tape recordings that provide a complete course of study in melodic and harmonic dictation, sightsinging, and aural harmonic analysis. The four volumes are:

I. INTERVALS
II. MELODY AND RHYTHM
III. CHORDS, Part I
IV. CHORDS, Part II

The flexibility of the program makes it suitable for use in any kind of theory program. The volumes may be used singly or as a group, alone or in combination with other text materials. Except for Volume IV, which depends on Volume III, they need not be taken sequentially; experience has shown, in fact, that for some students it is more profitable to work in several volumes concurrently.

Because the course is programed, the student works entirely on his own, at his own pace. Multiple copies of each written lesson are provided, so that he can repeat lessons as often as necessary to improve his skills. As he reaches recommended levels of proficiency, he takes tests, which are provided separately to the instructor and administered under his direction. A guide to the administration and grading of the program is provided in the Instructor's Manual.

PROGRAMED EAR TRAINING was developed at West Virginia University over a seven-year period during which it was in continuous use and was constantly being revised. It has also been used at more than a dozen other colleges and universities across the country; thus it has been thoroughly tested on large and varying groups of students.

The authors would like to express appreciation to Dr. Guy Bockmon, University of Tennessee, for his careful reading of all the materials and for his most helpful recommendations; to Dr. Richard E. Duncan, Dean of the Creative Arts Center, West Virginia University, who suggested and supported the project in which these books were developed; to Dr. Frank Lorince, Chairman of the Theory Department, West Virginia University, for his valuable advice and assistance; to the teachers who have used the books and offered suggestions and criticism, and finally to the many students who have worked patiently or otherwise through the program and whose reactions were always useful.

L.H.
G.L.

Contents

INTRODUCTION

This is the second of four volumes designed to help you improve your hearing and notational skills through techniques of programed instruction. Volume II is devoted to rhythmic and melodic skills in sightsinging and dictation. For each lesson in this volume there is a tape recording that provides all the audio material you will need to complete the lesson.

Programed instruction differs from usual instruction in two ways: first, most of the work can be done with little or no help from a teacher; and second, you can progress at your own rate. Where the material is difficult for you, you can move slowly. Where you find it easy, you can move rapidly, saving time and work. A faculty advisor will probably direct and guide your work, but the responsibility for making progress is yours. Through your test scores and your scores on each lesson, you will always know how well you are progressing.

The basic idea of programed instruction is as follows. The material is broken into small units called *frames*. In each frame, a small problem is presented and you will be asked to make a response. Immediately after you have made this response, the correct answer is provided so that you will know whether or not your response was correct. Through many confirmations of correct responses and correction of incorrect responses, complicated and difficult skills and concepts can be learned with ease. With the programed instruction procedures in this book, you will find that you can spend as little or as much time in any one area as you need.

For each lesson a goal has been set for you, to show you whether you are ready to move on to the next lesson. If you complete a lesson with no more than the number of errors indicated in the goal, move on to the next lesson. Otherwise you are to repeat the lesson. For this purpose five copies of every worksheet that requires a written response are provided. If after five tries you have not brought the number of errors down to the limit set in the goal, move on to the next lesson anyway.

When you have done an entire series in this fashion, take the test on that series. You will take the tests on your own, but they will be graded by your instructor. The score you will receive on each test is a *weighted score*, which means that your raw score is multiplied by a factor to compensate for the length, difficulty, and importance of the series.

The evaluation of your work will depend on the total of all your test scores rather than on an average of these scores. Therefore every test you take, even if the score is low, can help raise your grade. If you return to a series for more work in that area, you may retake the test and count the highest grade you make on that test. To help you know how well you are doing, three *achievement levels* are provided for each test.

The *first level* represents a very high degree of learning. Generally, when you achieve this level you should not expect to return to the material in the series but should spend your time on other material.

The *second level* represents a moderate achievement. The material in the series can be considered to be reasonably well learned, but if time permits or if you wish to raise your grade, it would be practical to return to the series for further work.

The *third level* represents a rather low but nevertheless significant amount of learning. You should at some time return to the series for further work.

Normally, it is most advantageous to move on from one series to the next regardless of the test scores, and then at certain points in the course, go back and do further work on any series on which your test score was lower than you would like. The most profitable pattern of moving on and working back varies from student to student, and it will be best to seek the advice of your instructor when you are undecided.

The *test record sheet* that appears at the end of this volume indicates for each test the three achievement levels and the maximum possible score, and provides a convenient place to keep a record of your scores.

The skills developed through this course of study are extremely valuable in almost any musical activity. Not only are they important in performing music, but they can also help you to understand music you hear, to arrange and write music, and to discuss and learn more about music.

With the method of study used in these volumes, you will find that you can work to develop these skills in a manner best suited to your particular needs and abilities. You can move slowly where you find difficulties, change to a different phase of the course if your progress has slowed down, and work at maximum speed where your competencies are strongest. This modern approach to music theory can enable you to learn these very important skills in the most efficient manner possible.

Elementary Dictation—Rhythm

In this series, there are four *rhythmic dictation lessons*. The purpose of the rhythmic dictation lessons is to develop your ability to write the rhythm of melodies you hear. A printed worksheet and a tape recording are provided for each lesson. Each frame on the worksheet contains two parts, each ending with a double bar line. The first part consists of a space for your written response. The second part consists of a printed answer. To do each frame, start by shielding the answer with a piece of paper or a card. When you have heard the melody, stop the tape and write the rhythm. Then slide the shield to the right and compare your response with the printed answer. Circle each frame in which you make an error. Your goal is to complete each lesson with no more than eight circled frames. When you have done so, go on to the next lesson. Otherwise repeat the lesson until you reach the goal or until you have done the lesson five times, at which point you should go on to the next lesson regardless of your score.

In all the dictation lessons in this volume, consider your response correct if the notation represents the same rhythm as that of the printed answer. For example, 26 should be considered correct even where the printed answer is 27.

Before beginning a lesson, it would be useful to glance at the worksheet to observe the note values used in the answers.

When you have done this series, take Test B1.

B1-1 Rhythmic dictation
(Copy 1)

Shield the answer. Listen to the melody and write the rhythm; then check your response. Circle incorrect responses. Stop the tape between frames. Goal: No more than eight incorrect frames.

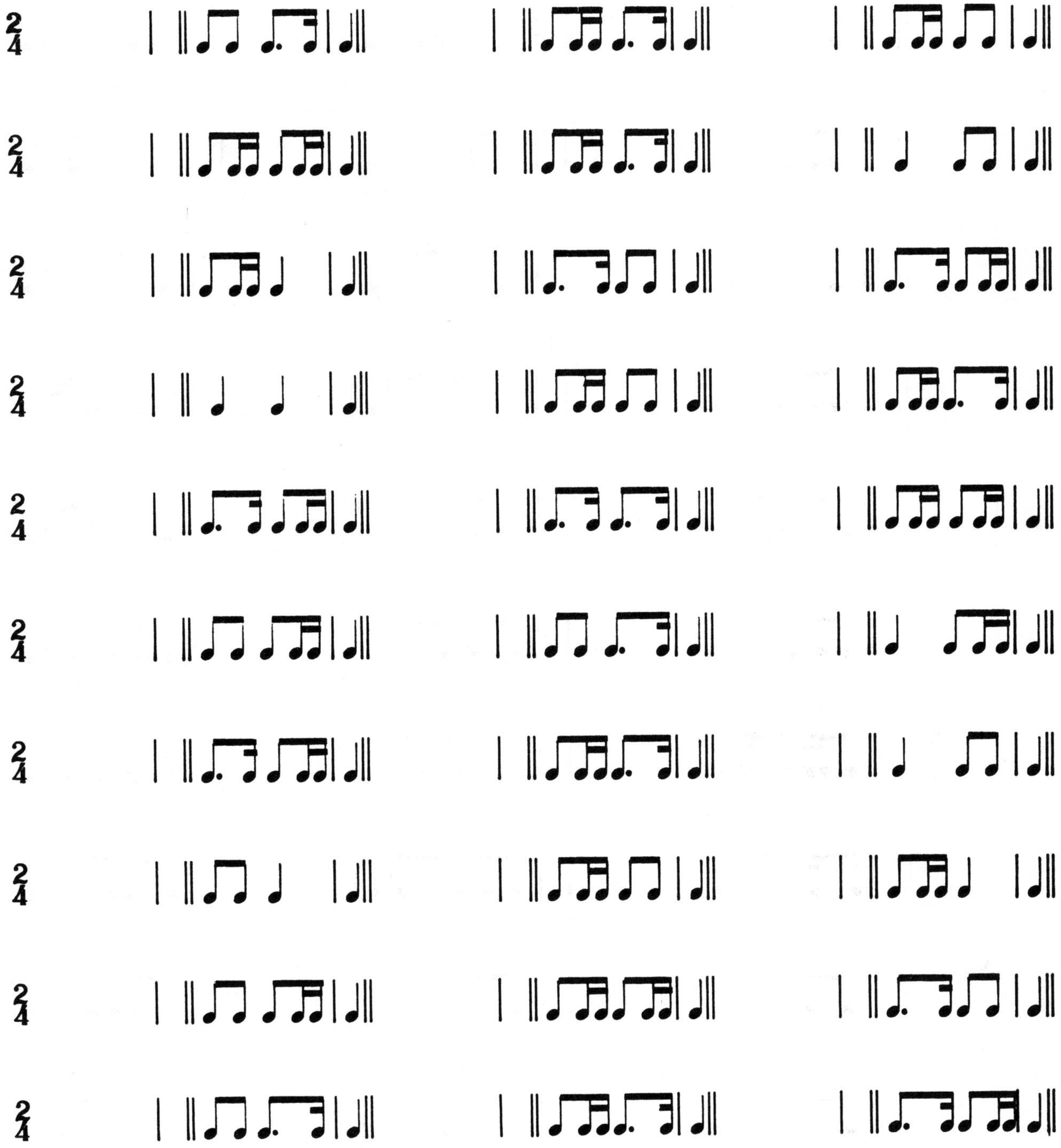

Rhythmic dictation

Shield the answer. Listen to the melody and write the rhythm; then check your response. Circle incorrect responses. Stop the tape between frames. Goal: No more than eight incorrect frames.

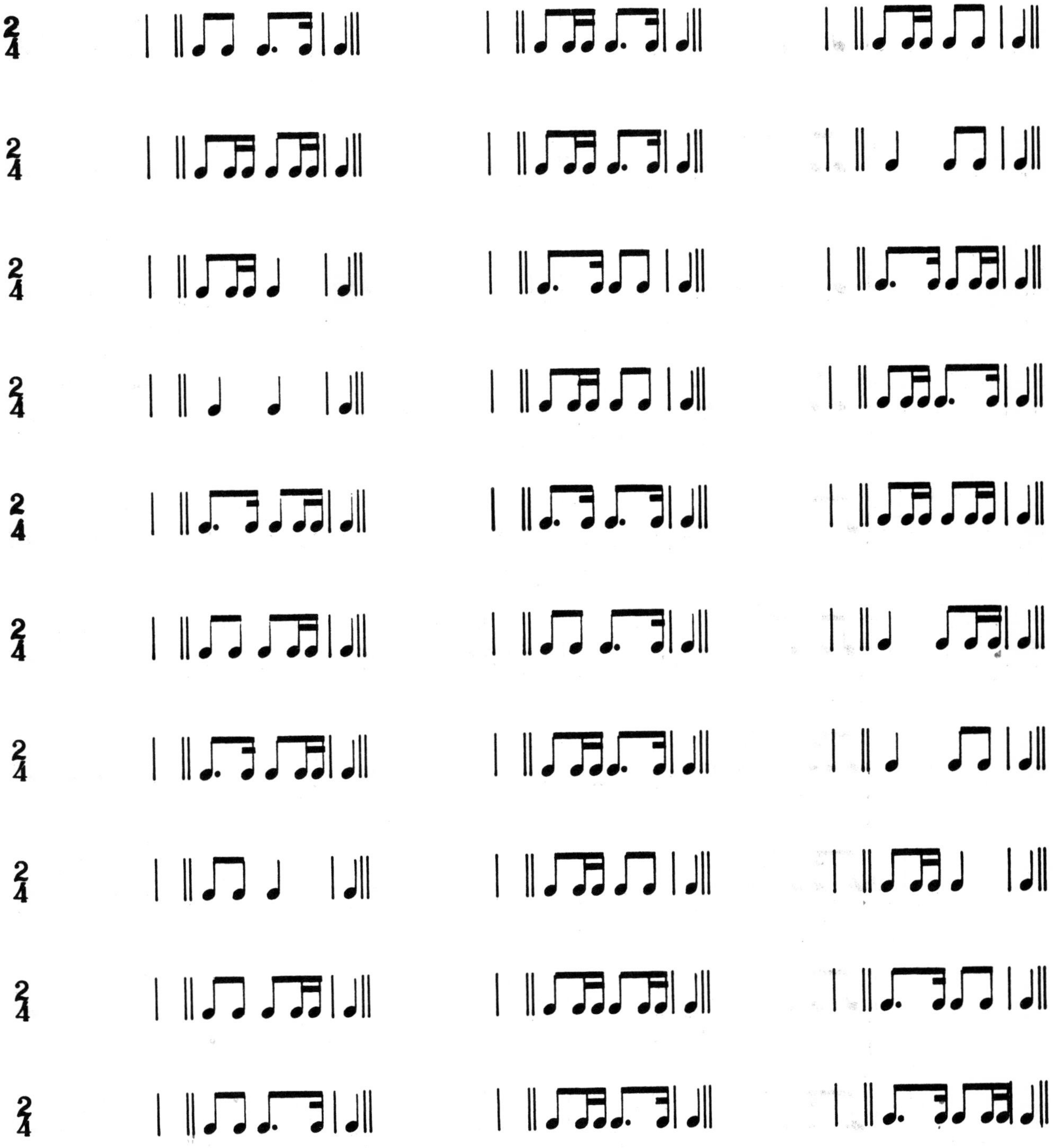

B1-1 Rhythmic dictation
(Copy 3)

Shield the answer. Listen to the melody and write the rhythm; then check your response. Circle incorrect responses. Stop the tape between frames. Goal: No more than eight incorrect frames.

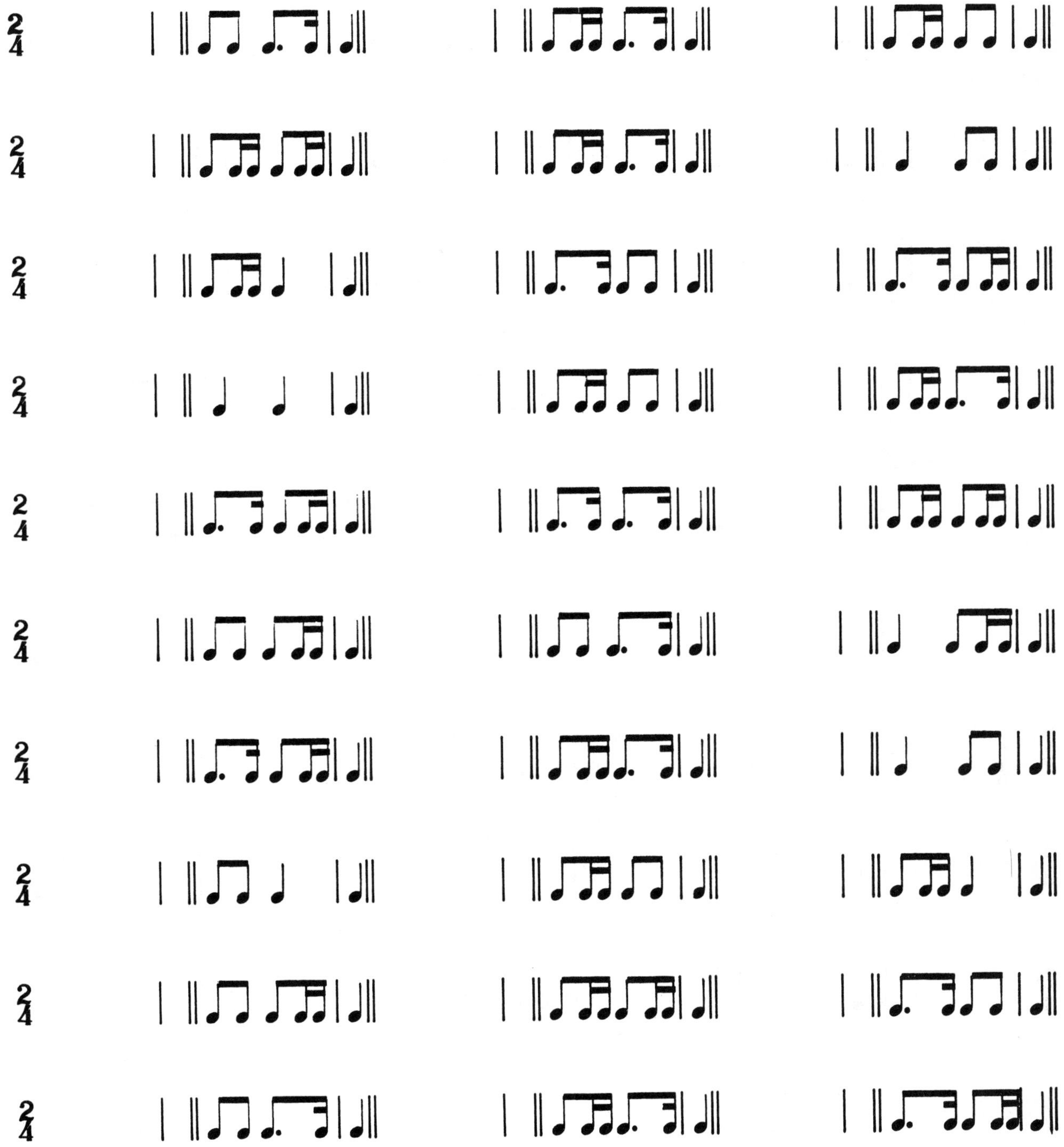

Rhythmic dictation

Shield the answer. Listen to the melody and write the rhythm; then check your response. Circle incorrect responses. Stop the tape between frames. Goal: No more than eight incorrect frames.

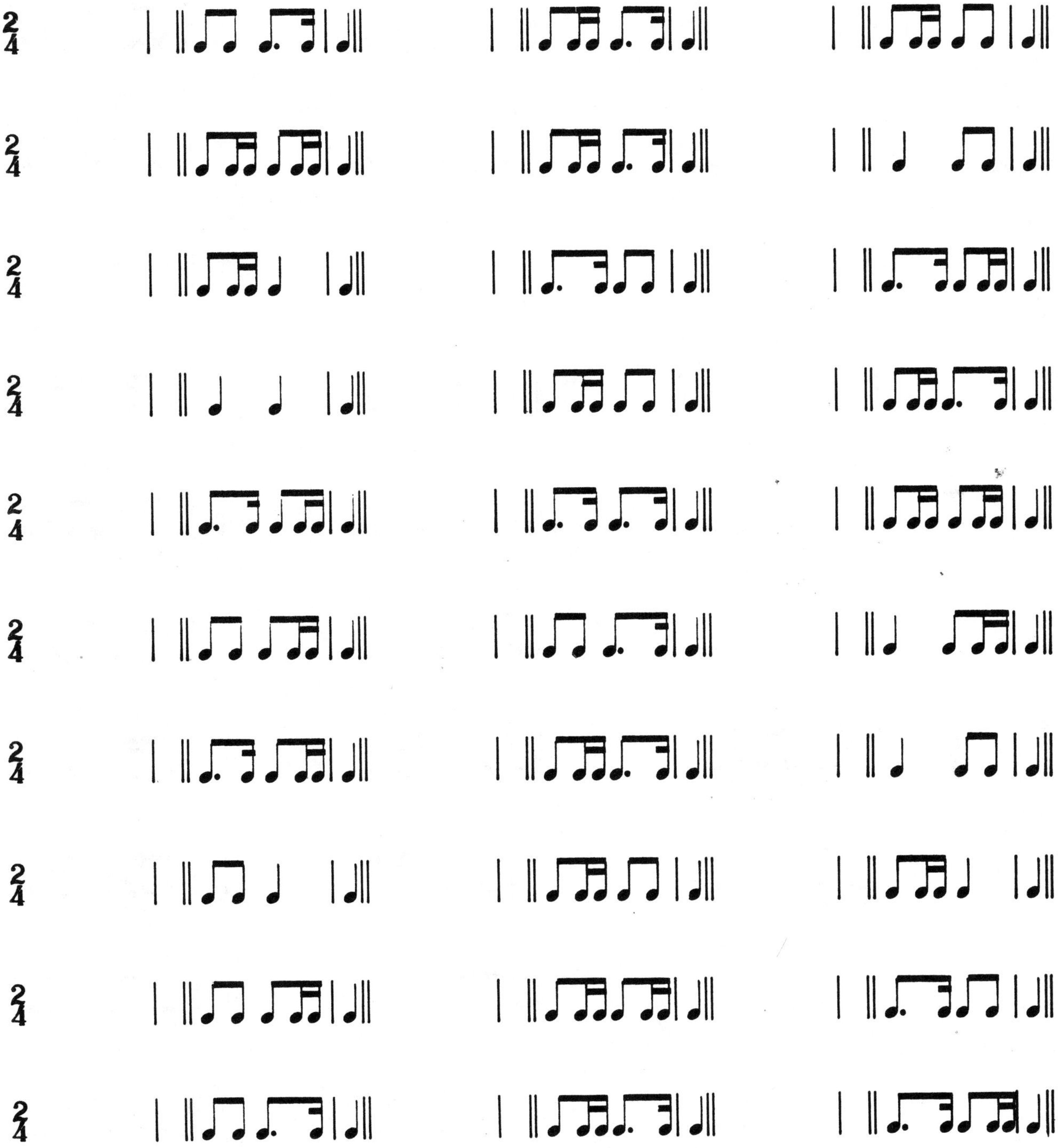

B1-1
(Copy 5)

Rhythmic dictation

Shield the answer. Listen to the melody and write the rhythm; then check your response. Circle incorrect responses. Stop the tape between frames. Goal: No more than eight incorrect frames.

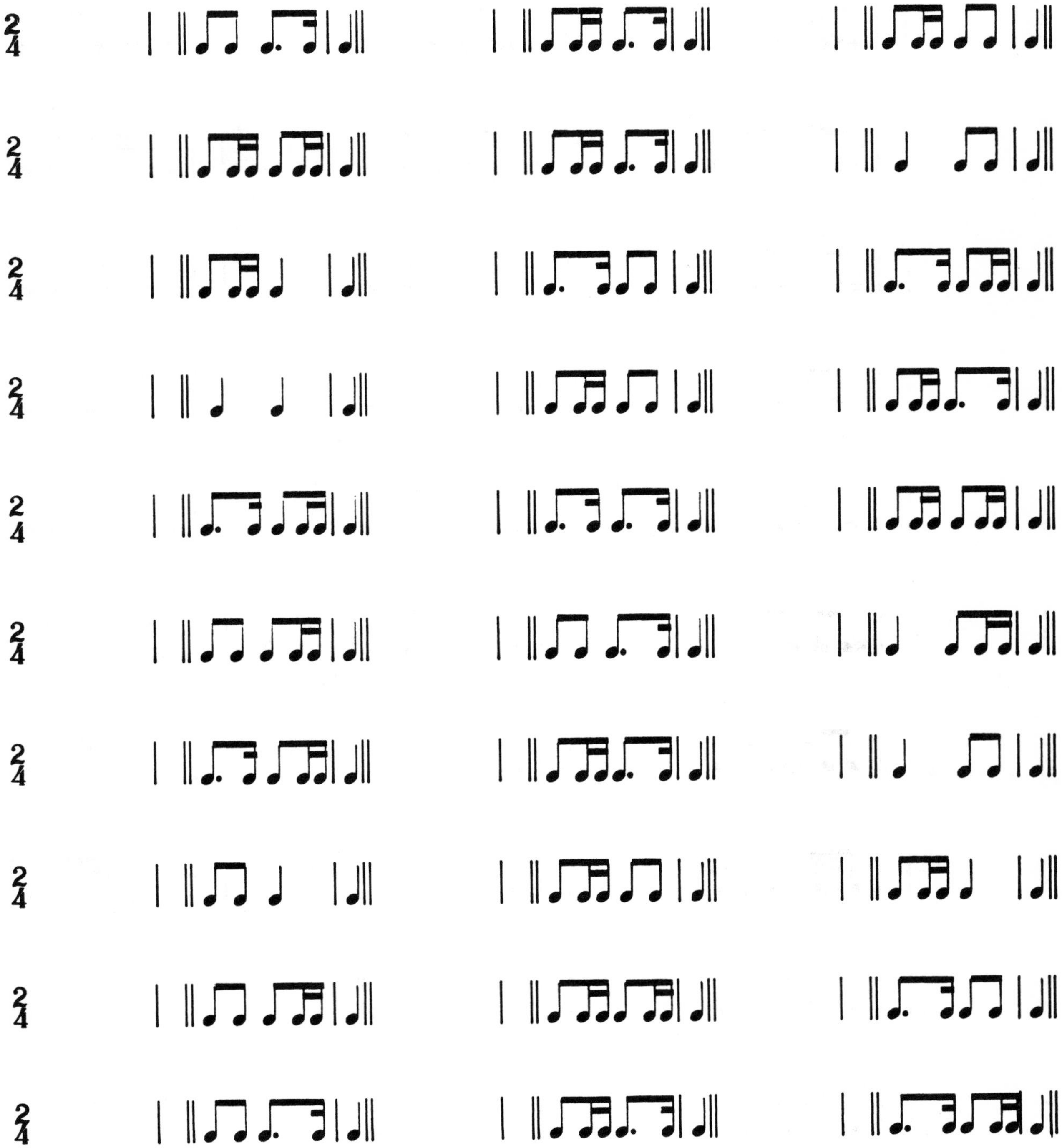

B1-2
(Copy 1)

Rhythmic dictation

Shield the answer. Listen to the melody and write the rhythm; then check your response. Circle incorrect responses. Stop the tape between frames. Goal: No more than eight incorrect frames.

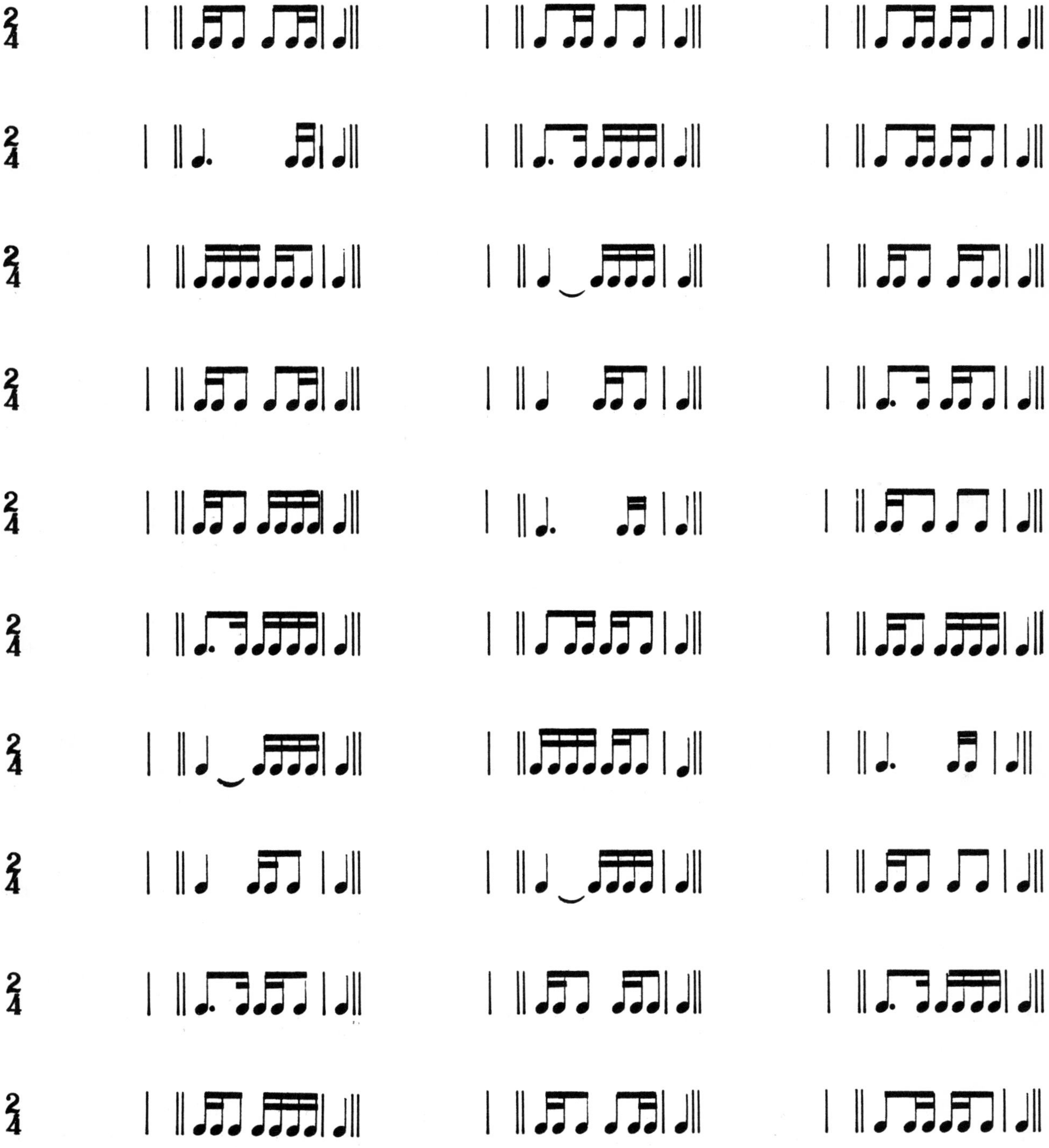

B1-2
(Copy 2)

Rhythmic dictation

Shield the answer. Listen to the melody and write the rhythm; then check your response. Circle incorrect responses. Stop the tape between frames. Goal: No more than eight incorrect frames.

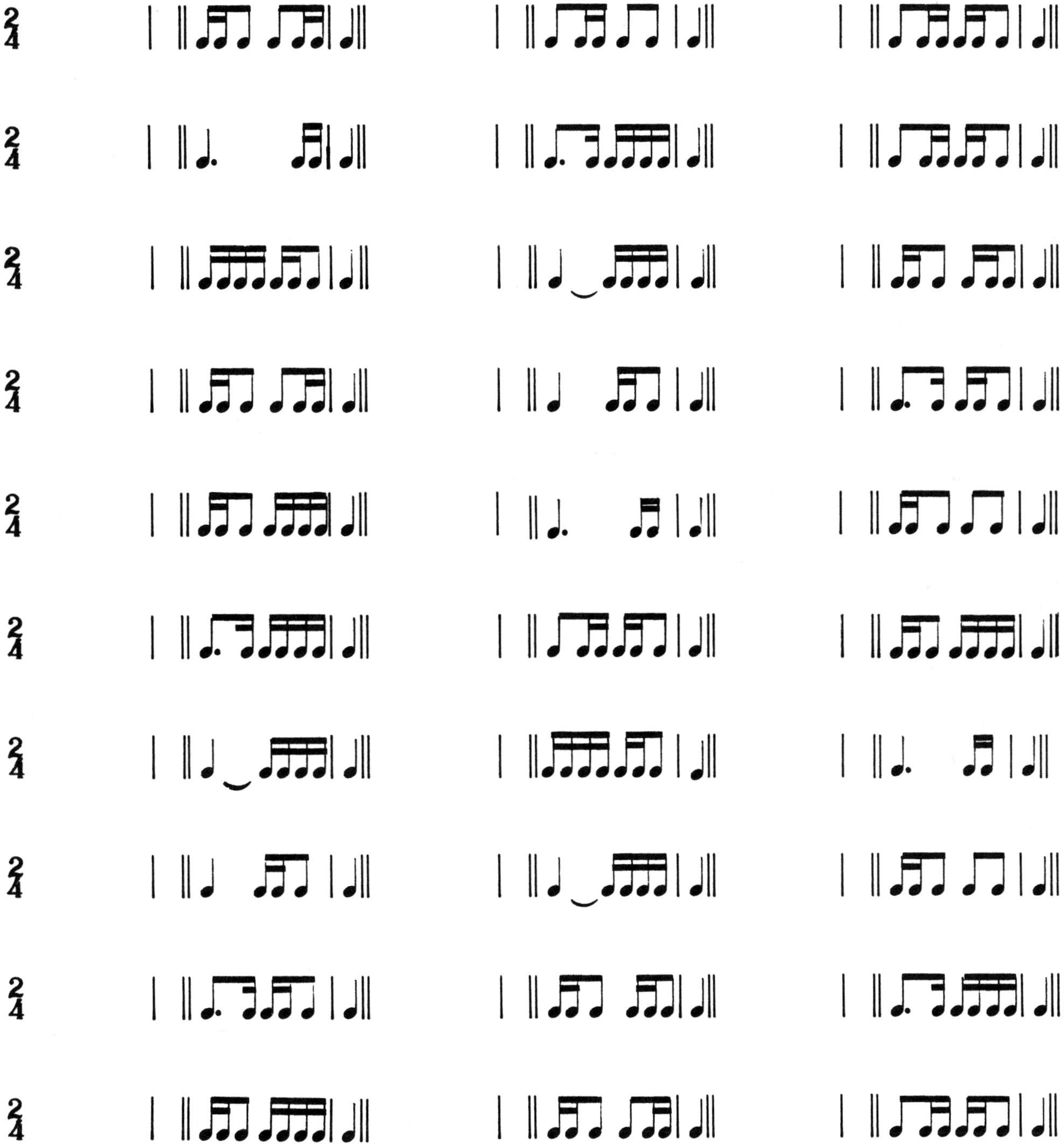
2/4

B1-2 Rhythmic dictation
(Copy 3)

Shield the answer. Listen to the melody and write the rhythm; then check your response. Circle incorrect responses. Stop the tape between frames. Goal: No more than eight incorrect frames.

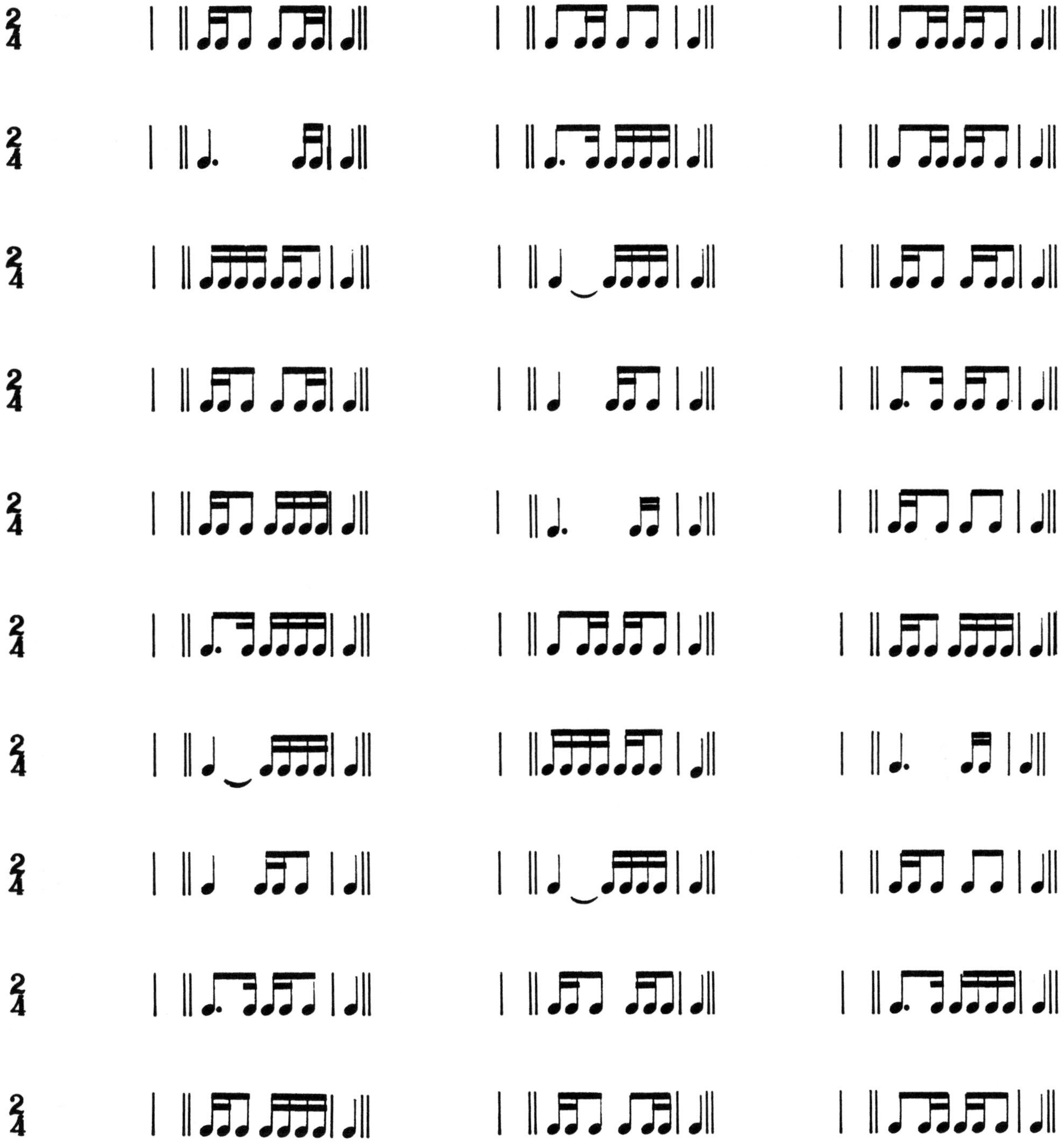

B1-2   Rhythmic dictation
(Copy 4)

Shield the answer. Listen to the melody and write the rhythm; then check your response. Circle incorrect responses. Stop the tape between frames. Goal: No more than eight incorrect frames.

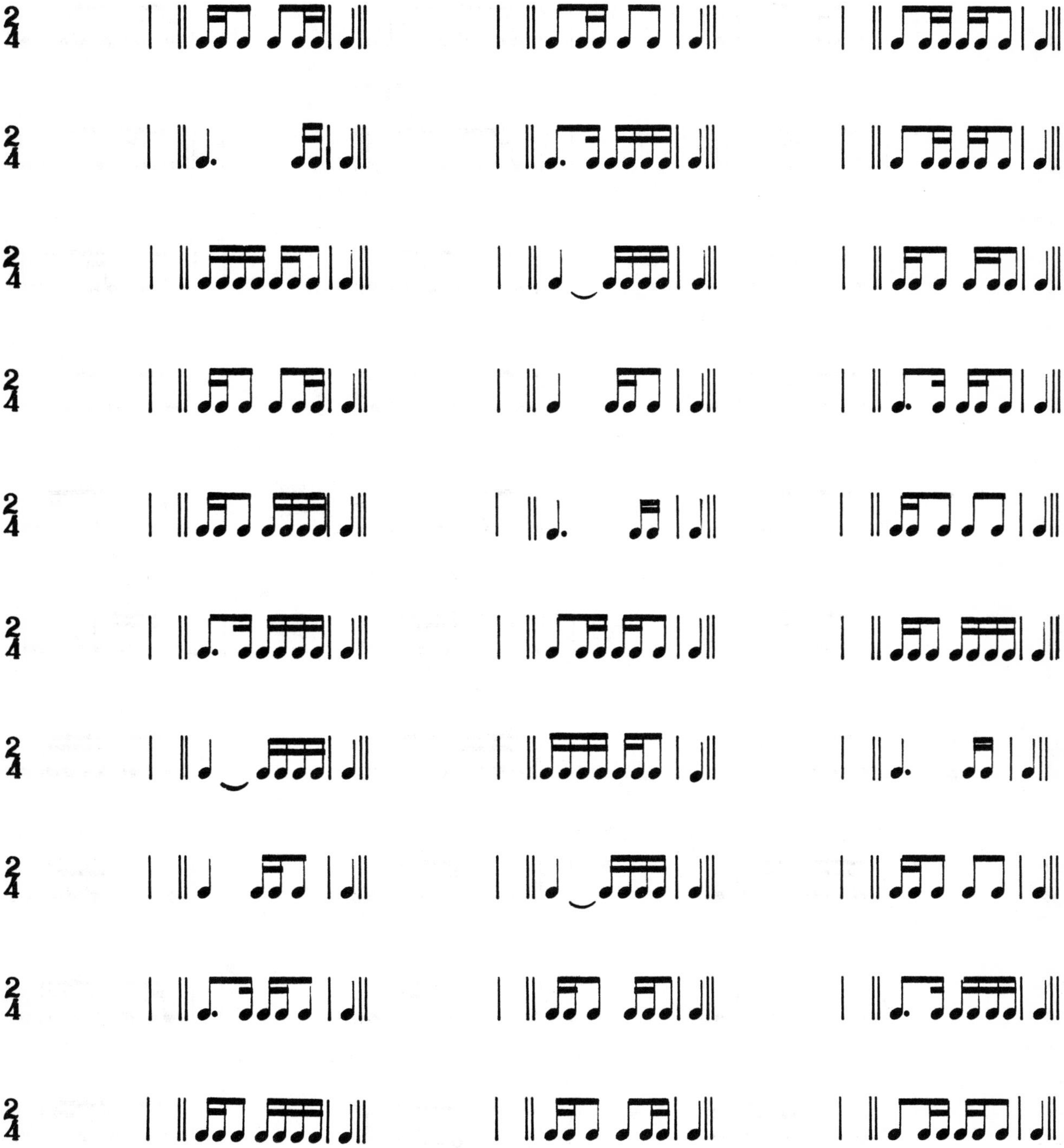

B1-2 **Rhythmic dictation**
(Copy 5)

Shield the answer. Listen to the melody and write the rhythm; then check your response. Circle incorrect responses. Stop the tape between frames. Goal: No more than eight incorrect frames.

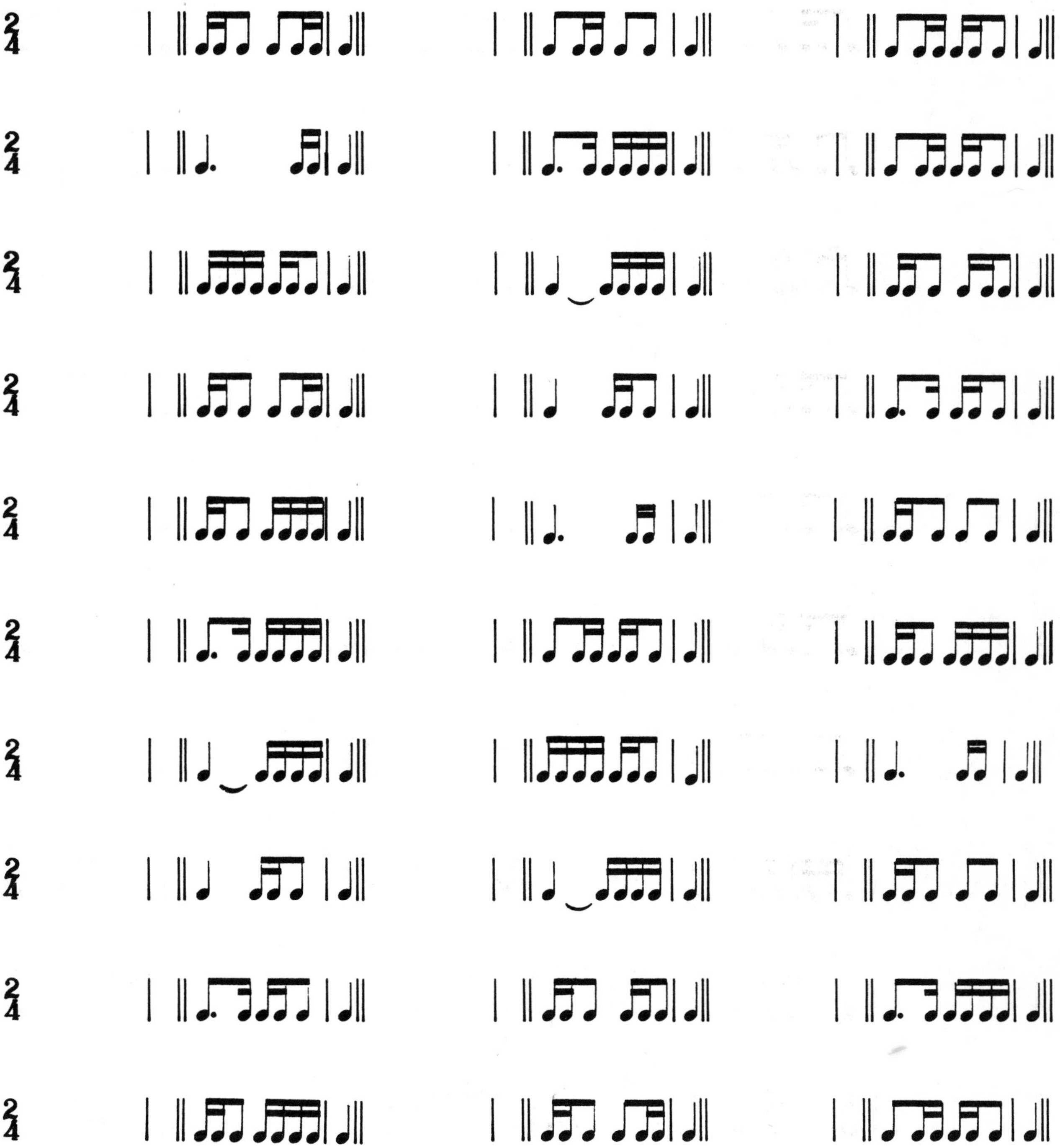

Rhythmic dictation

Shield the answer. Listen to the melody and write the rhythm; then check your response. Circle incorrect responses. Stop the tape between frames. Goal: No more than eight incorrect frames.

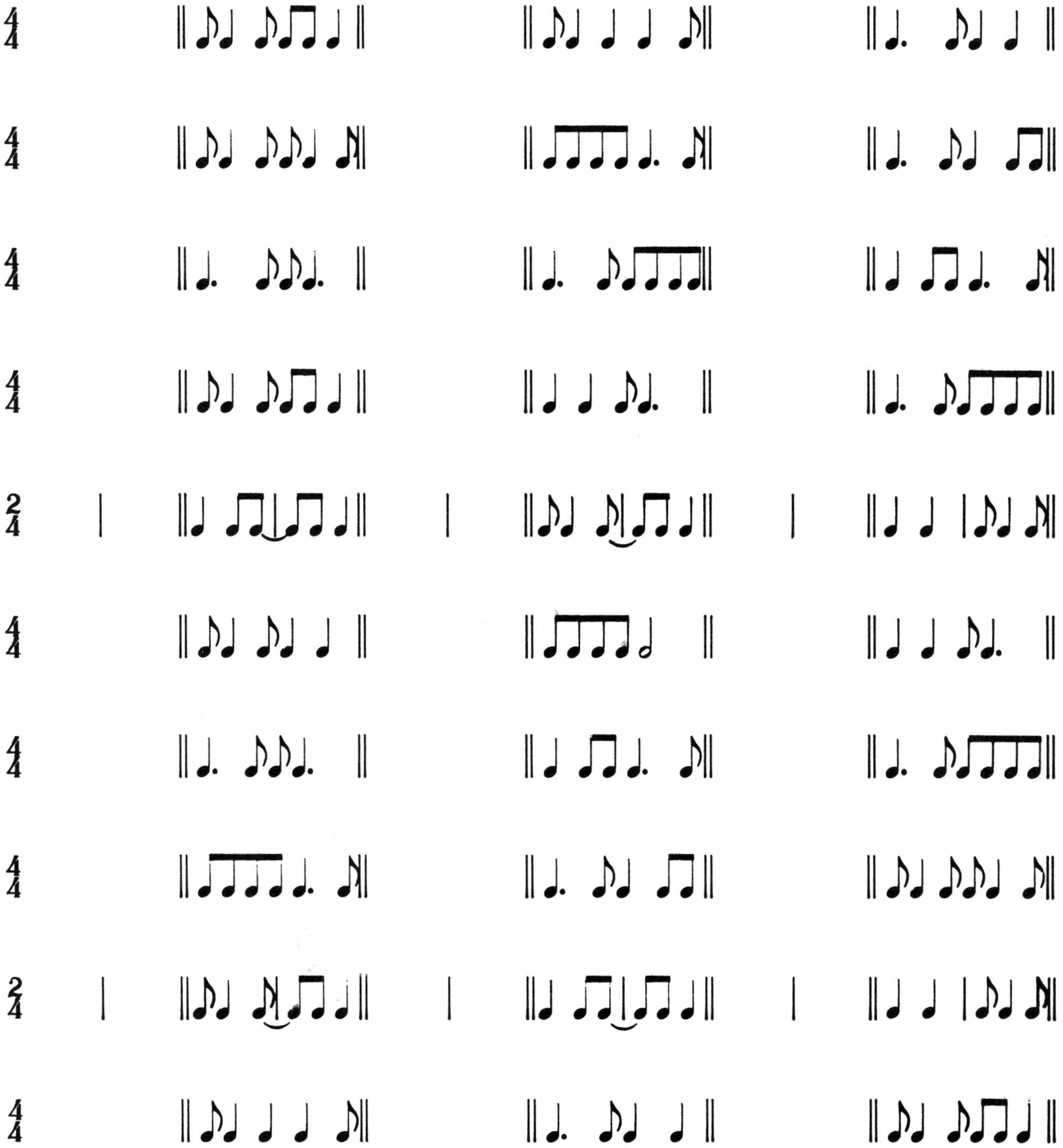

B1-3
(Copy 2)

Rhythmic dictation

Shield the answer. Listen to the melody and write the rhythm; then check your response. Circle incorrect responses. Stop the tape between frames. Goal: No more than eight incorrect frames.

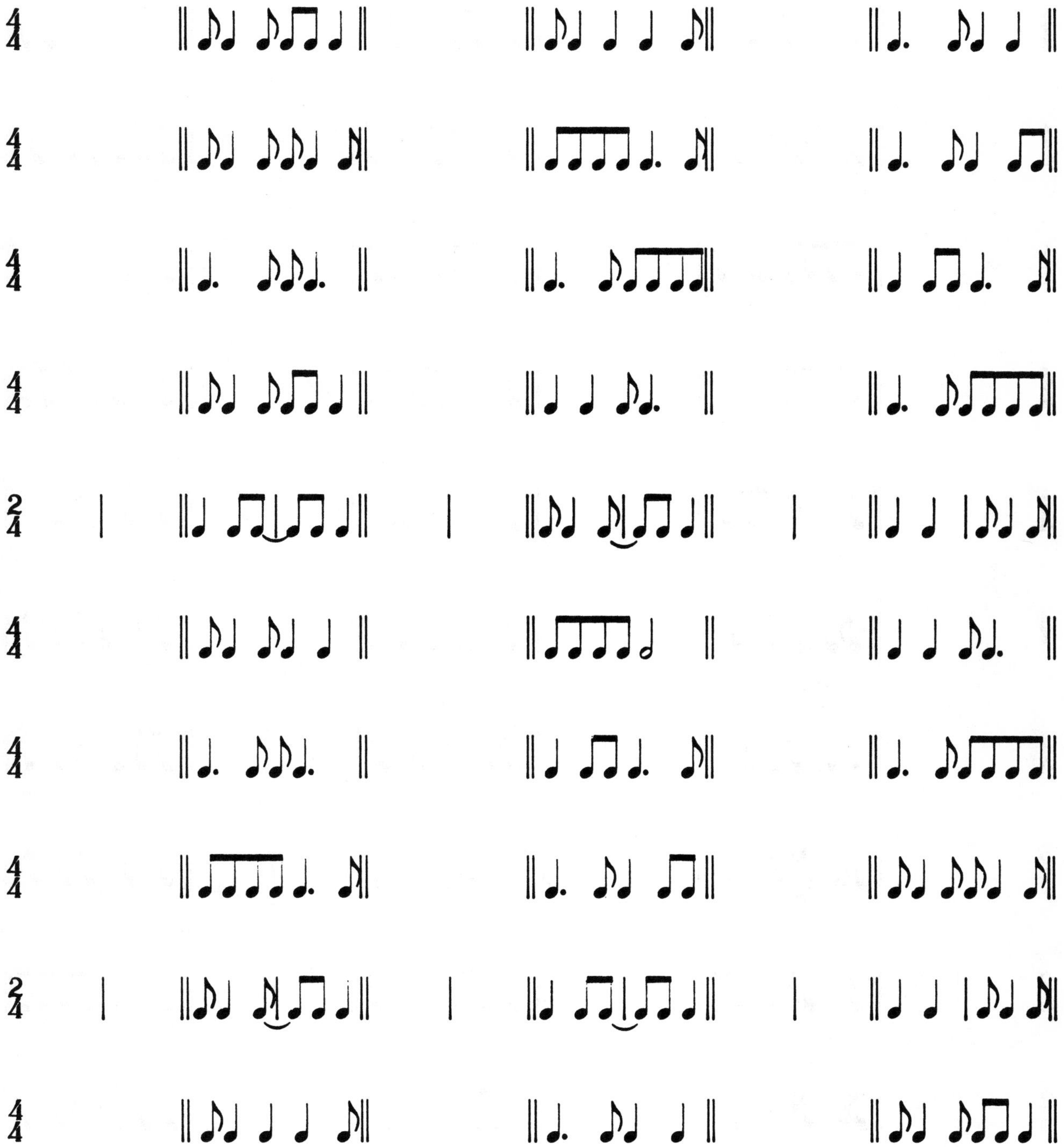

B1-3
(Copy 3)

Rhythmic dictation

Shield the answer. Listen to the melody and write the rhythm; then check your response. Circle incorrect responses. Stop the tape between frames. Goal: No more than eight incorrect frames.

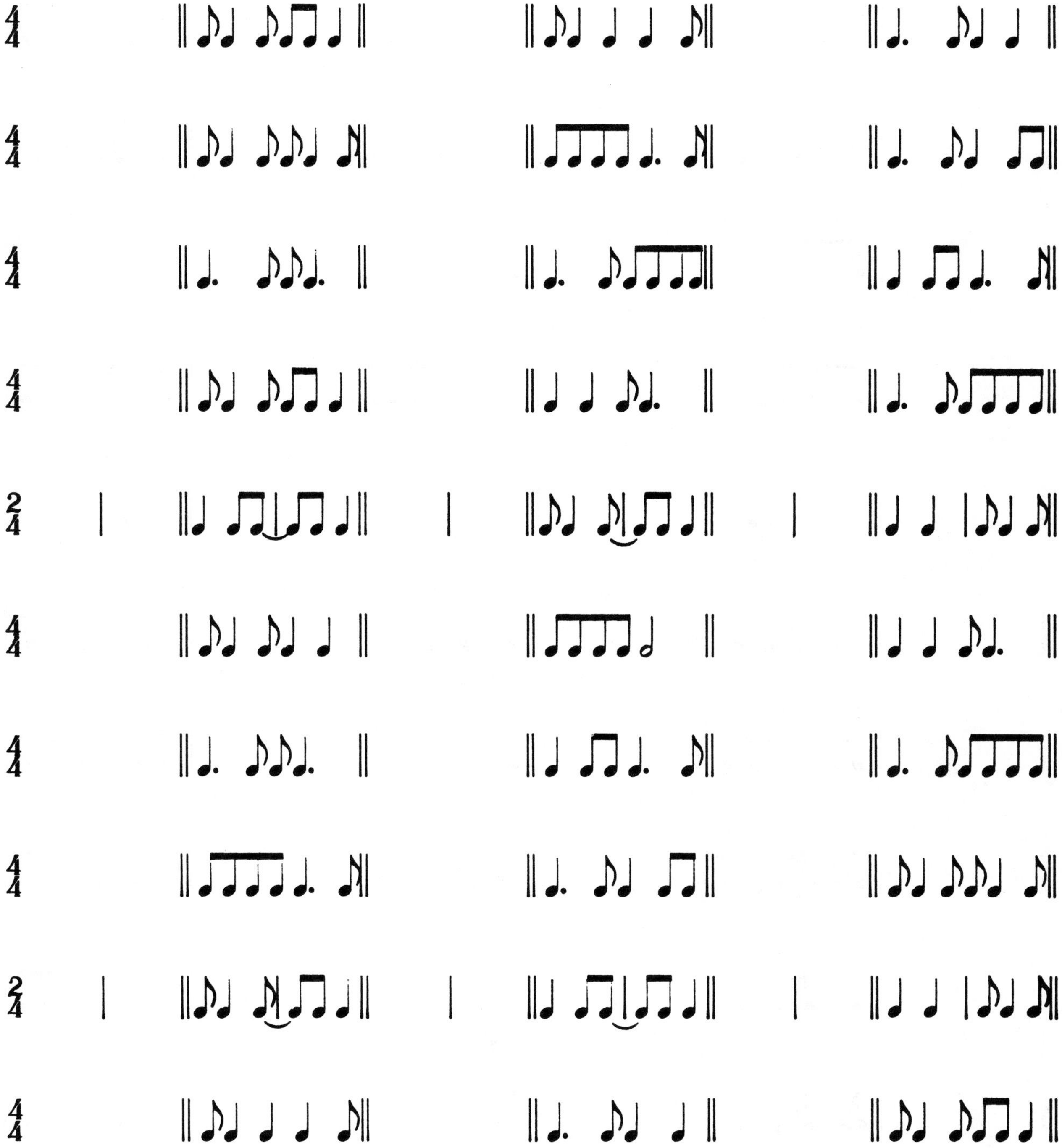
4/4
4/4
4/4
4/4
2/4
4/4
4/4
4/4
2/4
4/4

Shield the answer. Listen to the melody and write the rhythm; then check your response. Circle incorrect responses. Stop the tape between frames. Goal: No more than eight incorrect frames.

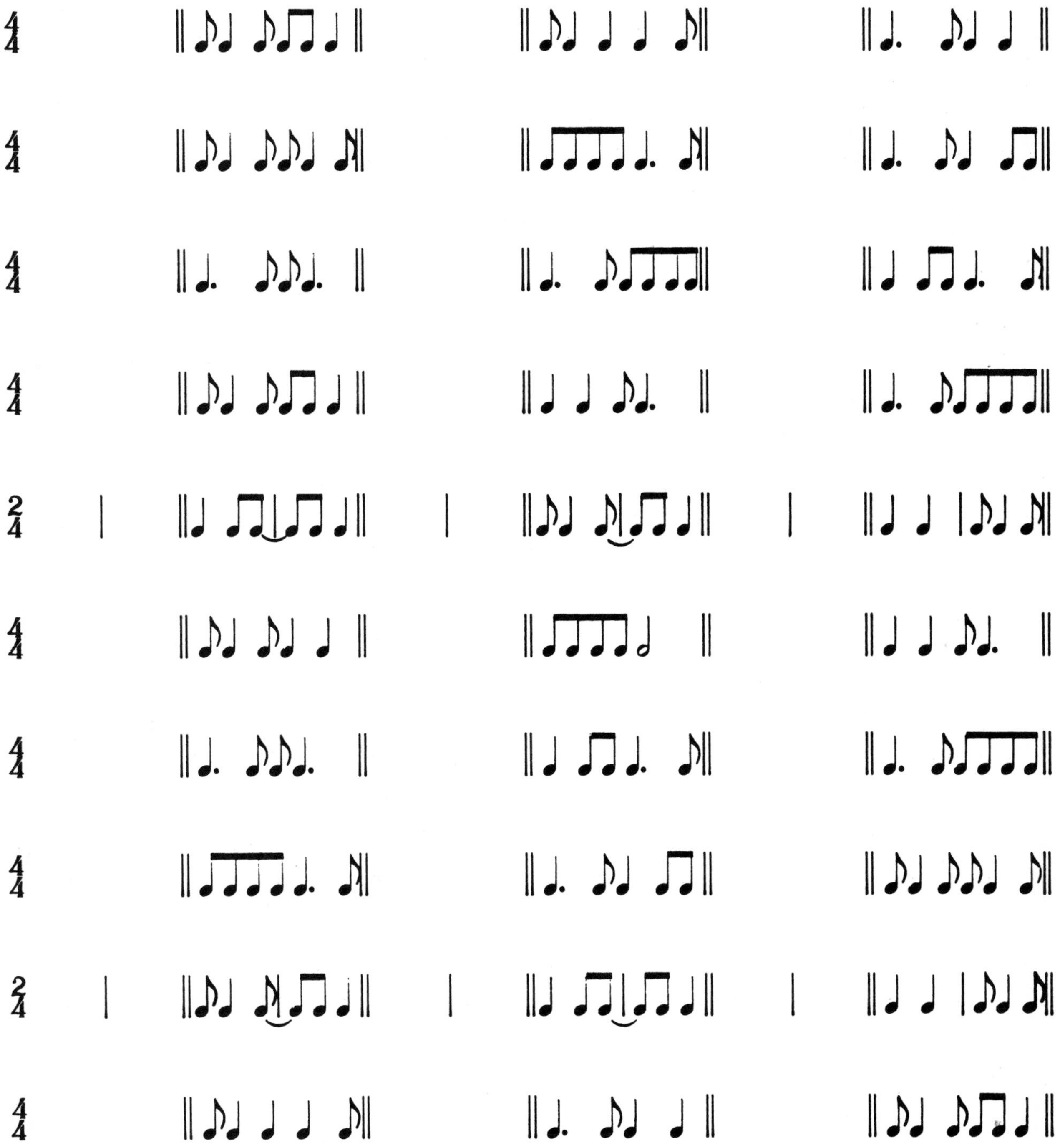

Rhythmic dictation

Shield the answer. Listen to the melody and write the rhythm; then check your response. Circle incorrect responses. Stop the tape between frames. Goal: No more than eight incorrect frames.

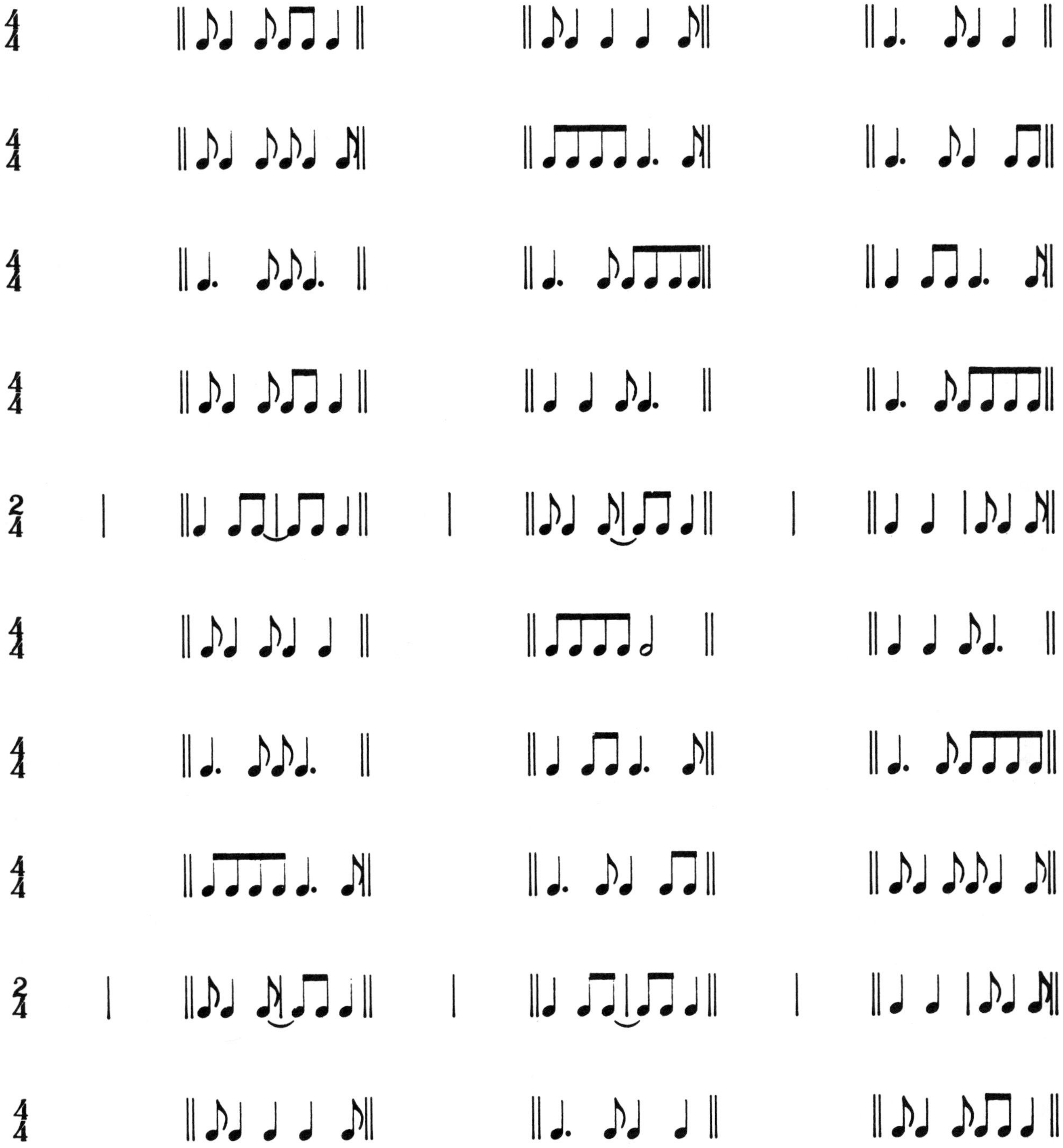

Rhythmic dictation

Shield the answer. Listen to the melody and write the rhythm; then check your response. Circle incorrect responses. Stop the tape between frames. Goal: No more than eight incorrect frames. After you have done this lesson, take Test B1.

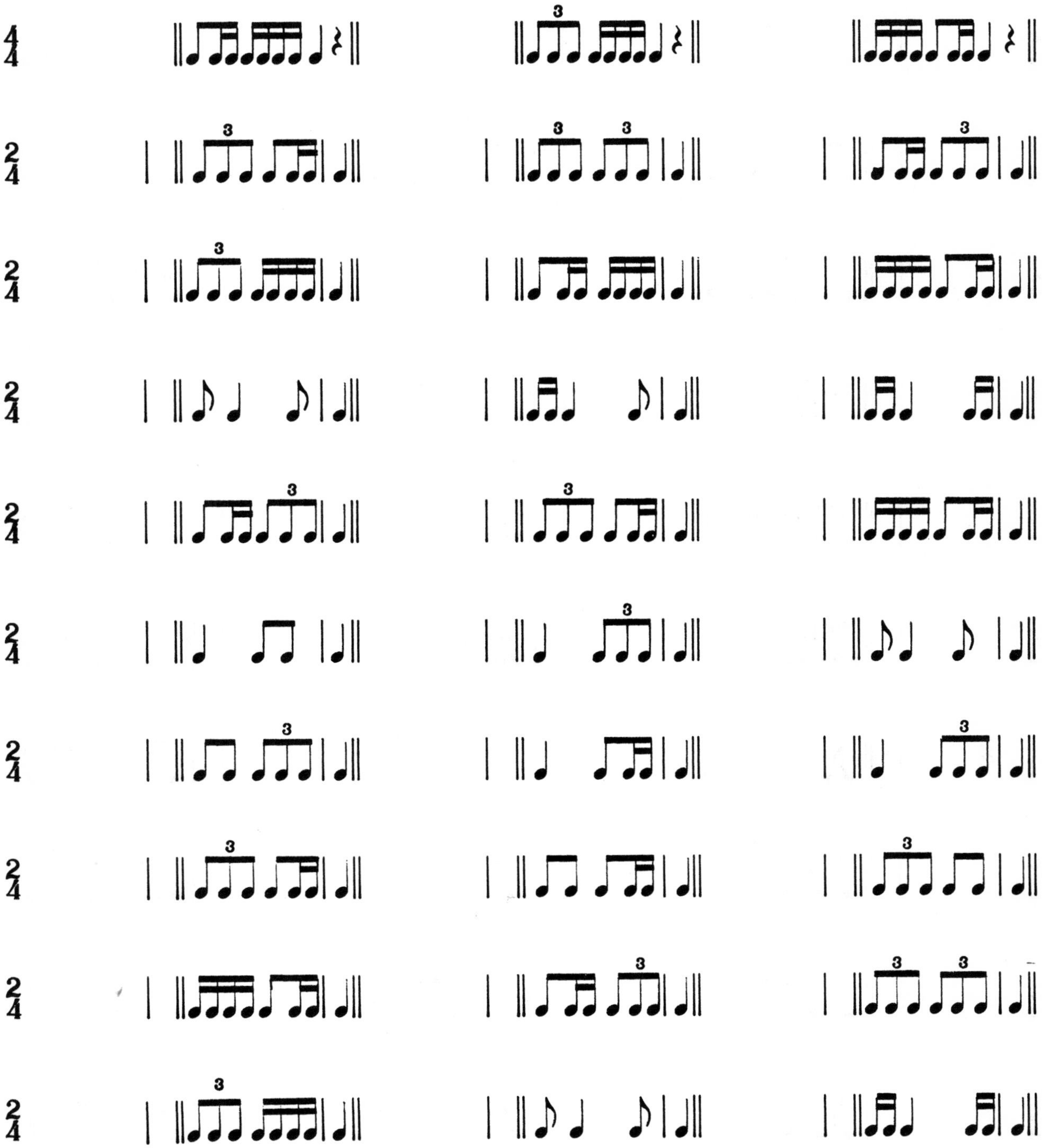

B1-4
(Copy 2)

Rhythmic dictation

Shield the answer. Listen to the melody and write the rhythm; then check your response. Circle incorrect responses. Stop the tape between frames. Goal: No more than eight incorrect frames. After you have done this lesson, take Test B1.

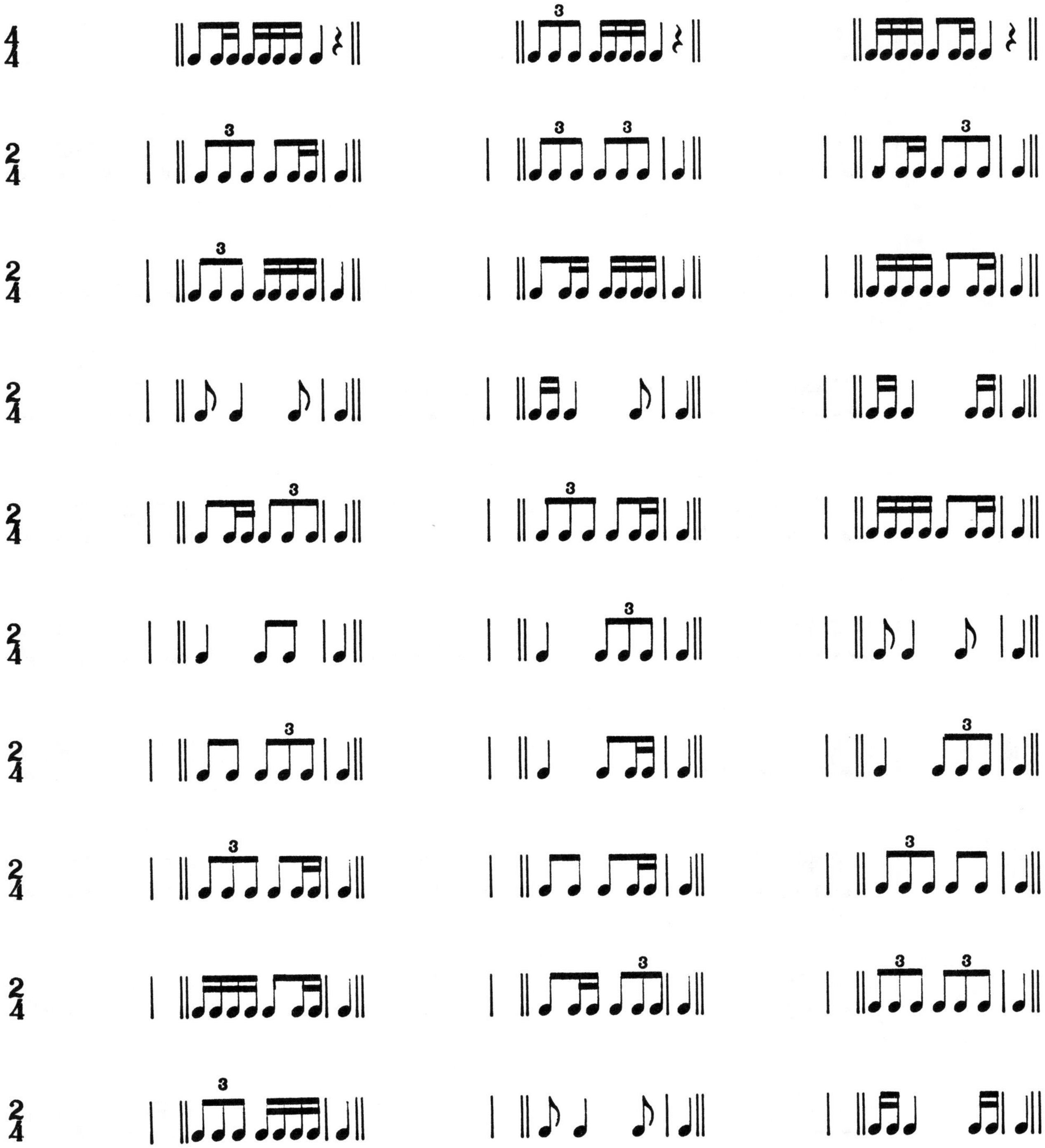

B1-4

(Copy 3)

Rhythmic dictation

Shield the answer. Listen to the melody and write the rhythm; then check your response. Circle incorrect responses. Stop the tape between frames. Goal: No more than eight incorrect frames. After you have done this lesson, take Test B1.

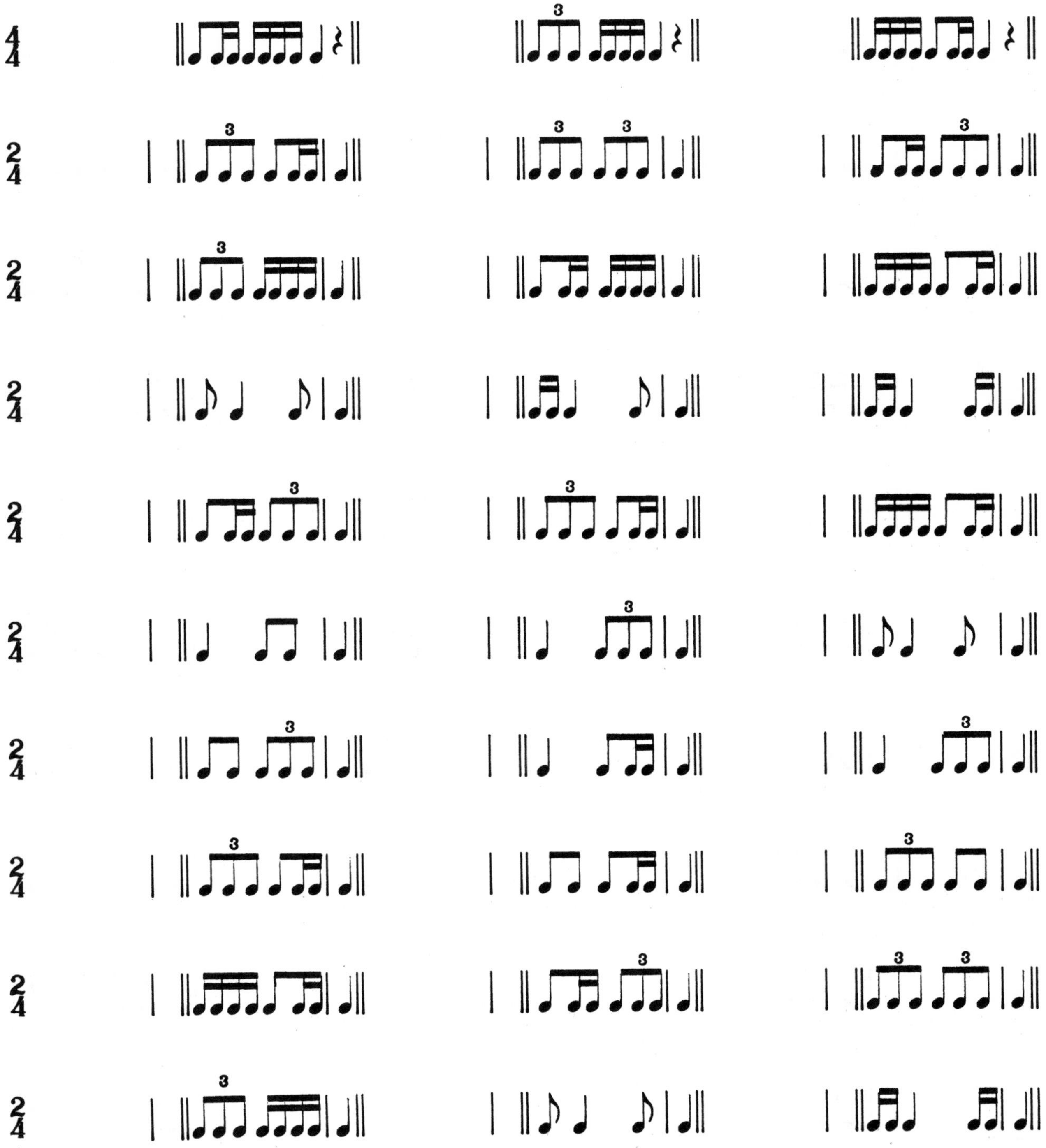

B1-4
(Copy 4)

Rhythmic dictation

Shield the answer. Listen to the melody and write the rhythm; then check your response. Circle incorrect responses. Stop the tape between frames. Goal: No more than eight incorrect frames. After you have done this lesson, take Test B1.

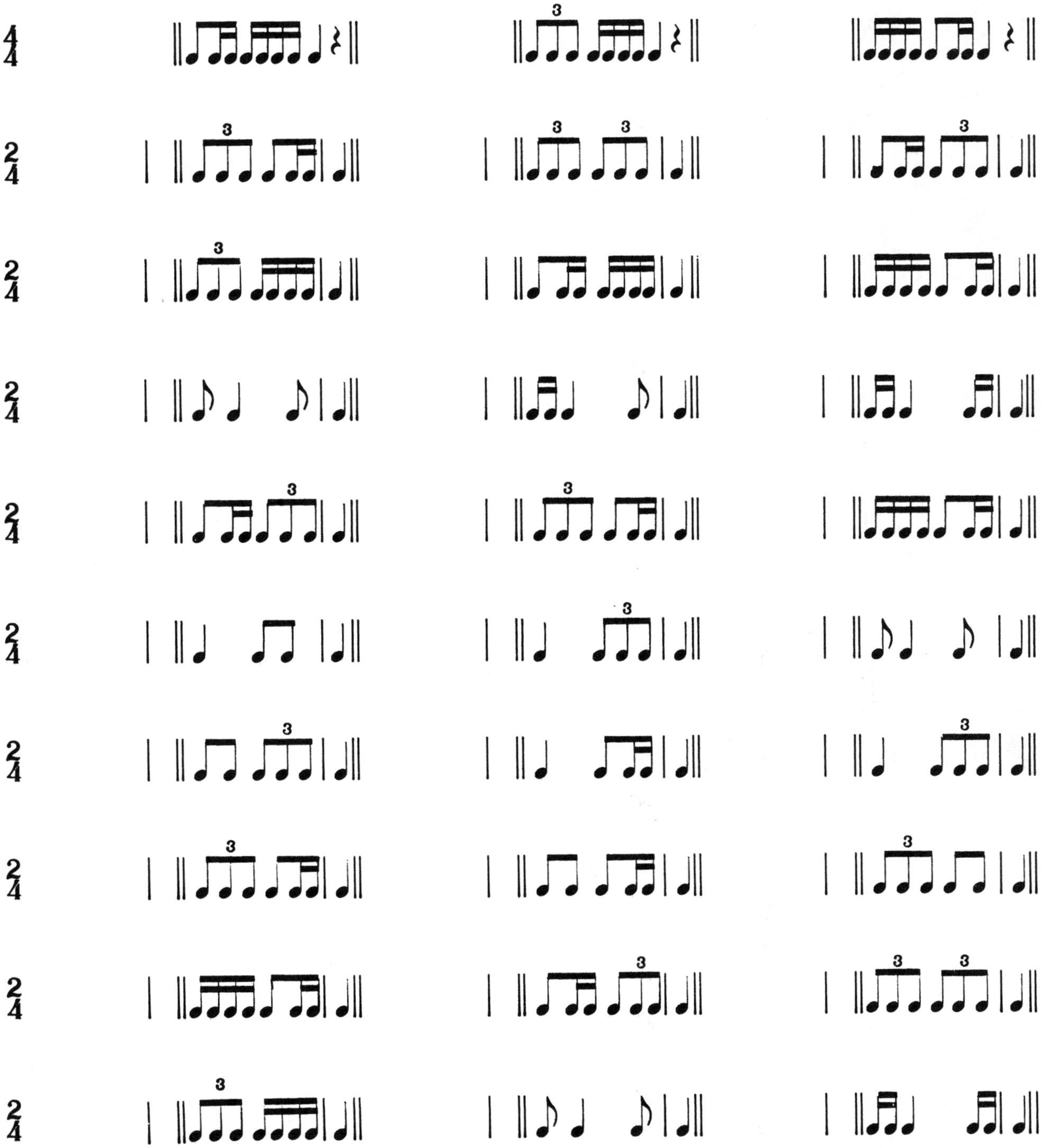

B1-4   Rhythmic dictation
(Copy 5)

Shield the answer. Listen to the melody and write the rhythm; then check your response. Circle incorrect responses. Stop the tape between frames. Goal: No more than eight incorrect frames. After you have done this lesson, take Test B1.

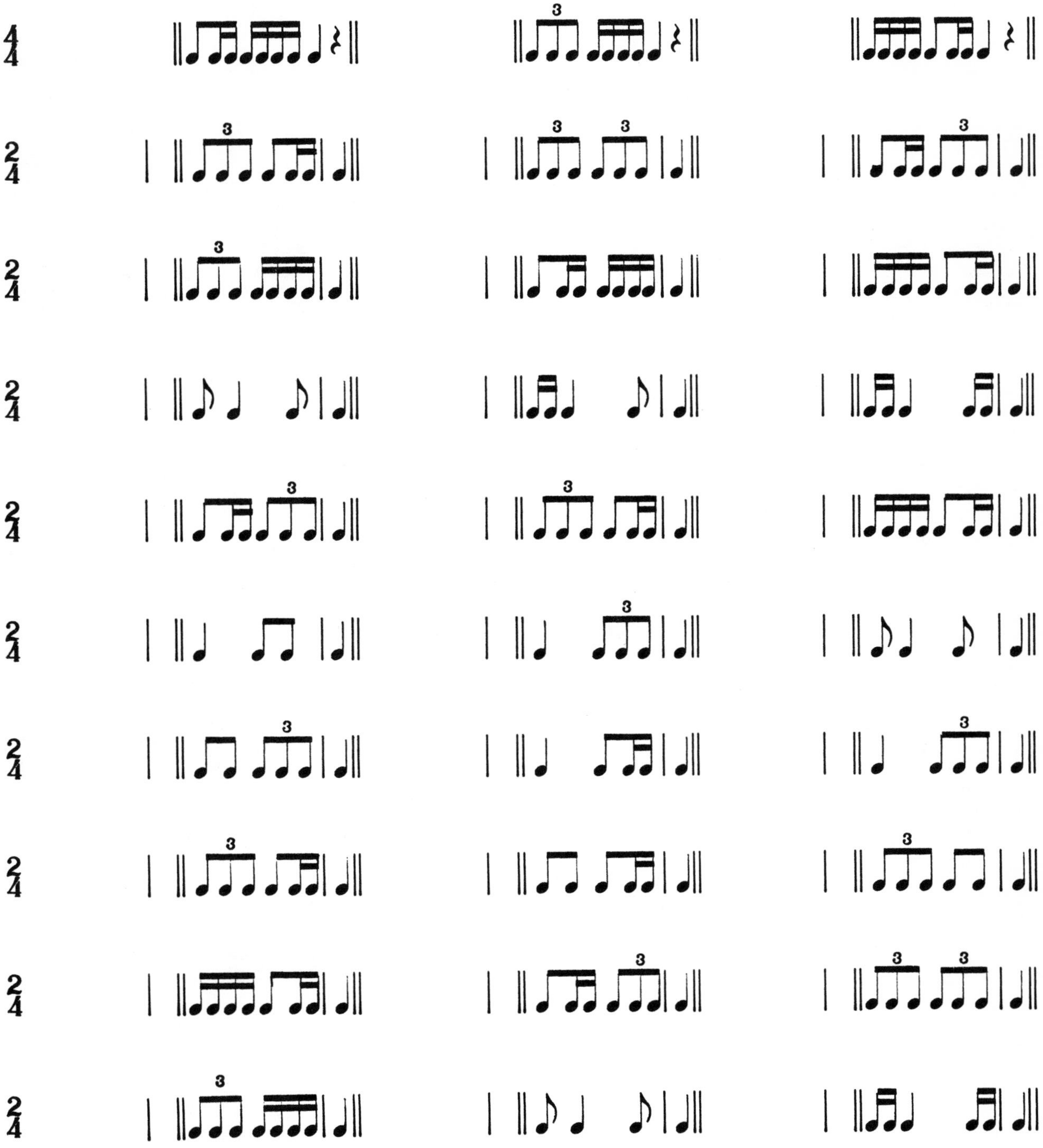

Elementary Sightsinging— Melody and Rhythm

SERIES B2

In this series there are seven *sightsinging lessons*. The following instructions apply to all lessons of this type in this volume.

The purpose of the sightsinging lessons is to develop your ability to sing melodies written in staff notation. A printed worksheet and a tape recording are provided for each lesson. The frames on the worksheet are separated by double bar lines. At the beginning of the tape recording you will hear a clicking metronome and the starting tone for the frame. After the starting tone, sing the printed melody in time with the metronome. You will then hear the melody correctly performed and will be able to determine whether your response was correct. Then sing the second frame and continue in the same fashion. For all frames except the first, you must find the starting tone yourself from the preceding frame. It is important to be quite critical as you compare your performance to the one you hear on the tape. Be sure that both the pitches and the rhythm you have sung are exactly like those on the tape. Whenever you sing a frame incorrectly, make a tally mark on a piece of paper. Your goal is to have no more than eight incorrect frames in an entire lesson. When you have reached this goal, go on to the next lesson. Otherwise repeat the lesson until you reach the goal or until you have done the lesson five times, at which point you should go on to the next lesson regardless of the number of errors.

Depending upon the range of your voice, you may find it necessary to sing in an octave different from that of the tones you hear on the tape recording. You may also find it necessary to change octaves in the course of the lesson. Sing in the most comfortable part of your vocal range at all times.

When you have done this series, take Test B2.

B2-1 Sightsinging

Sing each frame in time with the metronome and compare your response with the melody you then hear. The starting tone is given for the first frame only. Tally errors on a separate sheet of paper. Goal: No more than eight incorrect frames.

47

B2-2 Sightsinging

Sing each frame in time with the metronome and compare your response with the melody you then hear. The starting tone is given for the first frame only. Tally errors on a separate sheet of paper. Goal: No more than eight incorrect frames.

48

49

B2-3 Sightsinging

Sing each frame in time with the metronome and compare your response with the melody you then hear. The starting tone is given for the first frame only. Tally errors on a separate sheet of paper. Goal: No more than eight incorrect frames.

51

B2-4 Sightsinging

Sing each frame in time with the metronome and compare your response with the melody you then hear. The starting tone is given for the first frame only. Tally errors on a separate sheet of paper. Goal: No more than eight incorrect frames.

53

B2-5 Sightsinging

Sing each frame in time with the metronome and compare your response with the melody you then hear. The starting tone is given for the first frame only. Tally errors on a separate sheet of paper. Goal: No more than eight incorrect frames.

55

B2-6 Sightsinging

Sing each frame in time with the metronome and compare your response with the melody you then hear. The starting tone is given for the first frame only. Tally errors on a separate sheet of paper. Goal: No more than eight incorrect frames.

56

B2-7 Sightsinging

Sing each frame in time with the metronome and compare your response with the melody you then hear. The starting tone is given for the first frame only. Tally errors on a separate sheet of paper. Goal: No more than eight incorrect frames. After you have done this lesson take Test B2.

58

59

Elementary Dictation— Melody and Rhythm

In this series there are four *melodic dictation lessons*. The following instructions apply to all lessons labeled *melodic dictation lessons.*

   The purpose of the dictation lessons is to develop your ability to write melodies which you hear. A printed worksheet and a tape recording are provided for each lesson. Each frame on the worksheet contains two parts, each part ending with a double bar line. In the first part, you will find a notehead for the first tone and space for your written response. In the second part, you will find the printed answer. To do each frame, start by shielding the answer with a piece of paper or a card. When you have heard the melody, stop the tape and notate it. Then slide the shield to the right and compare your response with the printed answer. Circle each frame in which you make an error. Your goal is to complete each lesson with no more than eight circled frames. When you have done so, go on to the next lesson. Otherwise repeat the lesson until you reach the goal or until you have done the lesson five times, at which point you should go on to the next lesson regardless of the number of errors.

   When you have done this series, take Test B3.

B3-1 Melodic dictation

(Copy 1)

Shield the answer. Listen to the melody and notate it; then check your response. Circle incorrect responses. Stop the tape between frames. Goal: No more than eight incorrect frames.

63

64

B3-1 Melodic dictation

(Copy 2)

Shield the answer. Listen to the melody and notate it; then check your response. Circle incorrect responses. Stop the tape between frames. Goal: No more than eight incorrect frames.

66

67

B3-1

(Copy 3)

Melodic dictation

Shield the answer. Listen to the melody and notate it; then check your response. Circle incorrect responses. Stop the tape between frames. Goal: No more than eight incorrect frames.

70

B3-1 Melodic dictation

(Copy 4)

Shield the answer. Listen to the melody and notate it; then check your response. Circle incorrect responses. Stop the tape between frames. Goal: No more than eight incorrect frames.

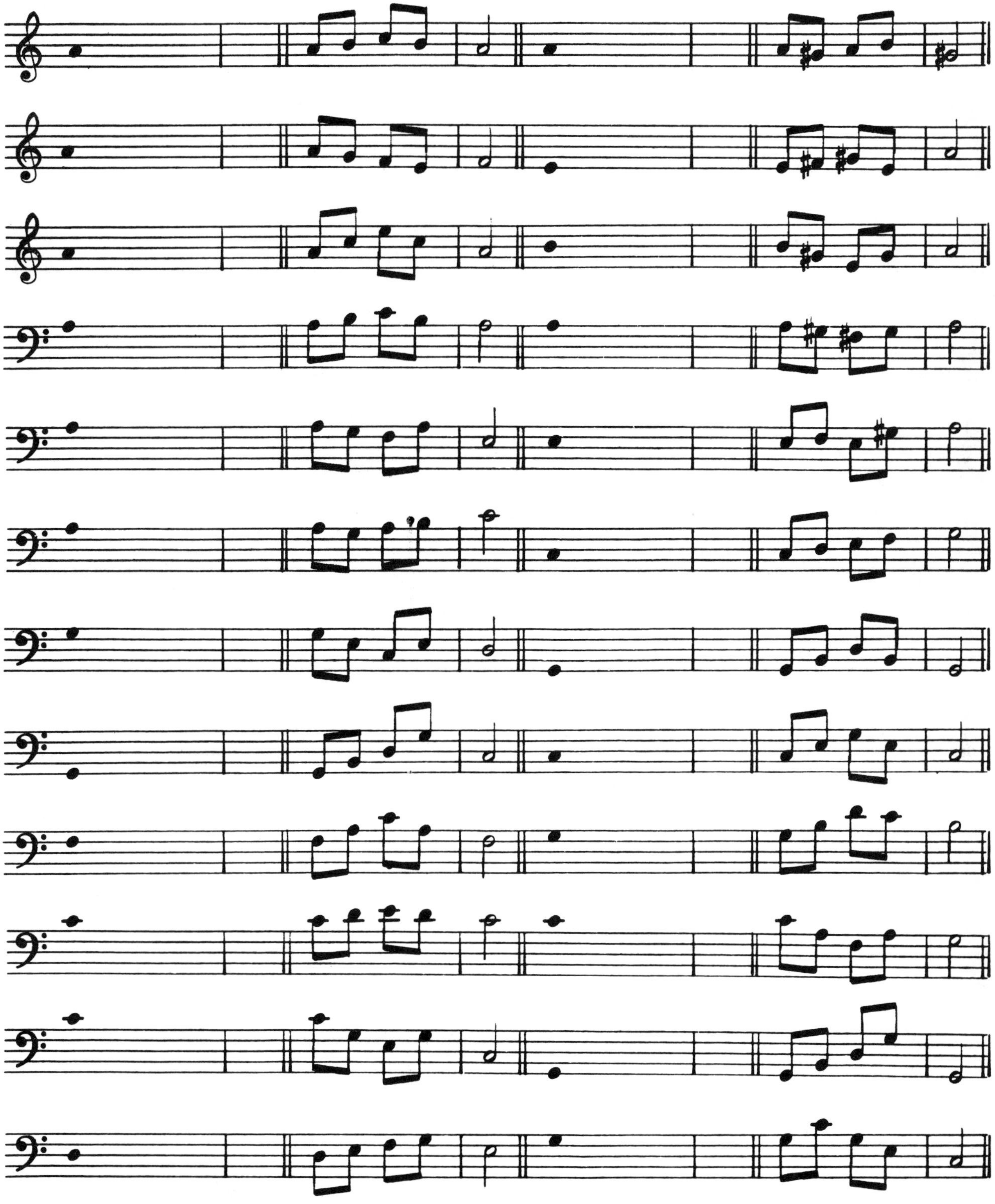

B3-1 Melodic dictation
(Copy 5)

Shield the answer. Listen to the melody and notate it; then check your response. Circle incorrect responses. Stop the tape between frames. Goal: No more than eight incorrect frames.

76

B3-2

(Copy 1)

Melodic dictation

Shield the answer. Listen to the melody and notate it; then check your response. Circle incorrect responses. Stop the tape between frames. Goal: No more than eight incorrect frames.

78

79

B3-2 Melodic dictation

(Copy 2)

Shield the answer. Listen to the melody and notate it; then check your response. Circle incorrect responses. Stop the tape between frames. Goal: No more than eight incorrect frames.

81

82

B3-2 Melodic dictation

(Copy 3)

Shield the answer. Listen to the melody and notate it; then check your response. Circle incorrect responses. Stop the tape between frames. Goal: No more than eight incorrect frames.

83

84

85

B3-2

(Copy 4)

Melodic dictation

Shield the answer. Listen to the melody and notate it; then check your response. Circle incorrect responses. Stop the tape between frames. Goal: No more than eight incorrect frames.

87

88

B3-2

(Copy 5)

Melodic dictation

Shield the answer. Listen to the melody and notate it; then check your response. Circle incorrect responses. Stop the tape between frames. Goal: No more than eight incorrect frames.

91

B3-3
(Copy 1)

Melodic dictation

Shield the answer. Listen to the melody and notate it; then check your response. Circle incorrect responses. Stop the tape between frames. Goal: No more than eight incorrect frames.

93

B3-3 Melodic dictation

Shield the answer. Listen to the melody and notate it; then check your response. Circle incorrect responses. Stop the tape between frames. Goal: No more than eight incorrect frames.

95

97

B3-3
(Copy 3)

Melodic dictation

Shield the answer. Listen to the melody and notate it; then check your response. Circle incorrect responses. Stop the tape between frames. Goal: No more than eight incorrect frames.

99

100

B3-3

(Copy 4)

Melodic dictation

Shield the answer. Listen to the melody and notate it; then check your response. Circle incorrect responses. Stop the tape between frames. Goal: No more than eight incorrect frames.

102

103

B3-3 Melodic dictation

(Copy 5)

Shield the answer. Listen to the melody and notate it; then check your response. Circle incorrect responses. Stop the tape between frames. Goal: No more than eight incorrect frames.

105

106

B3-4 Melodic dictation

(Copy 1)

Shield the answer. Listen to the melody and notate it; then check your response. Circle incorrect responses. Stop the tape between frames. Goal: No more than eight incorrect frames. After you have done this lesson, take Test B3.

107

108

109

B3-4 Melodic dictation

(Copy 2)

Shield the answer. Listen to the melody and notate it; then check your response. Circle incorrect responses. Stop the tape between frames. Goal: No more than eight incorrect frames. After you have done this lesson, take Test B3.

110

111

B3-4 Melodic dictation

(Copy 3)

Shield the answer. Listen to the melody and notate it; then check your response. Circle incorrect responses. Stop the tape between frames. Goal: No more than eight incorrect frames. After you have done this lesson, take Test B3.

115

B3-4 Melodic dictation

Shield the answer. Listen to the melody and notate it; then check your response. Circle incorrect responses. Stop the tape between frames. Goal: No more than eight incorrect frames. After you have done this lesson, take Test B3.

116

118

B3-4

(Copy 5)

Melodic dictation

Shield the answer. Listen to the melody and notate it; then check your response. Circle incorrect responses. Stop the tape between frames. Goal: No more than eight incorrect frames. After you have done this lesson, take Test B3.

121

Intermediate Dictation—Rhythm

In this series there are four *rhythmic dictation lessons.* The procedure for these is the same as in Series B1: a printed worksheet and a tape recording are provided for each lesson. To do each frame, start by shielding the answer. When you have heard the melody, stop the tape and write the rhythm of the melody. Then slide the shield to the right and compare your response with the printed answer. Circle each frame in which your response is incorrect. Your goal is to complete each lesson with no more than eight incorrect frames. When you have done so, go on to the next lesson. If you have more than eight incorrect frames, repeat the lesson until you reach the goal or until you have done the lesson five times, at which point you should go on to the next lesson regardless of the number of errors.

When you have done this series, take Test B4.

B4-1　Rhythmic dictation
(Copy 1)

Shield the answer. Listen to the melody and write the rhythm; then check your response. Circle incorrect responses. Stop the tape between frames. Goal: No more than eight incorrect frames.

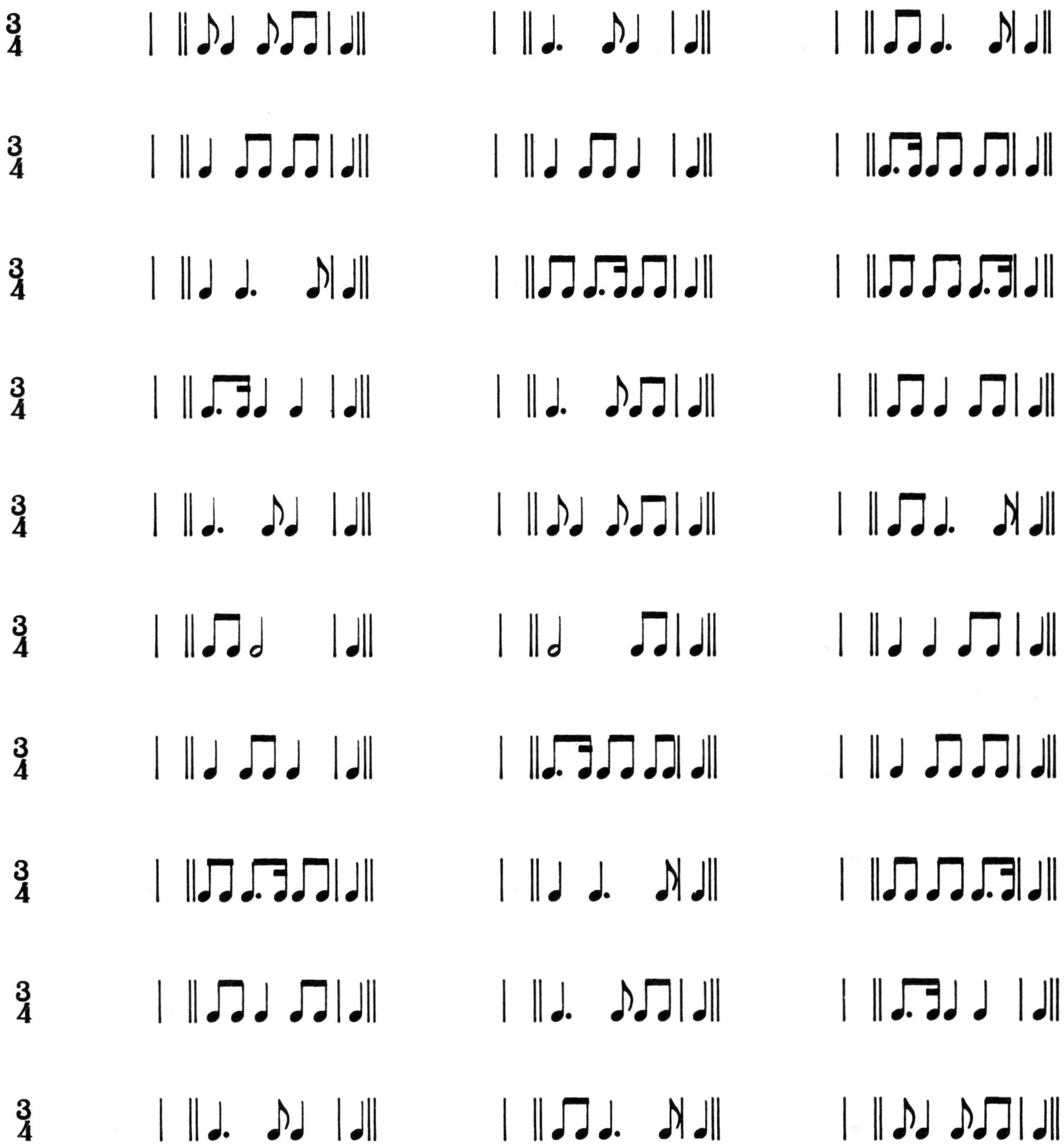

Rhythmic dictation

Shield the answer. Listen to the melody and write the rhythm; then check your response. Circle incorrect responses. Stop the tape between frames. Goal: No more than eight incorrect frames.

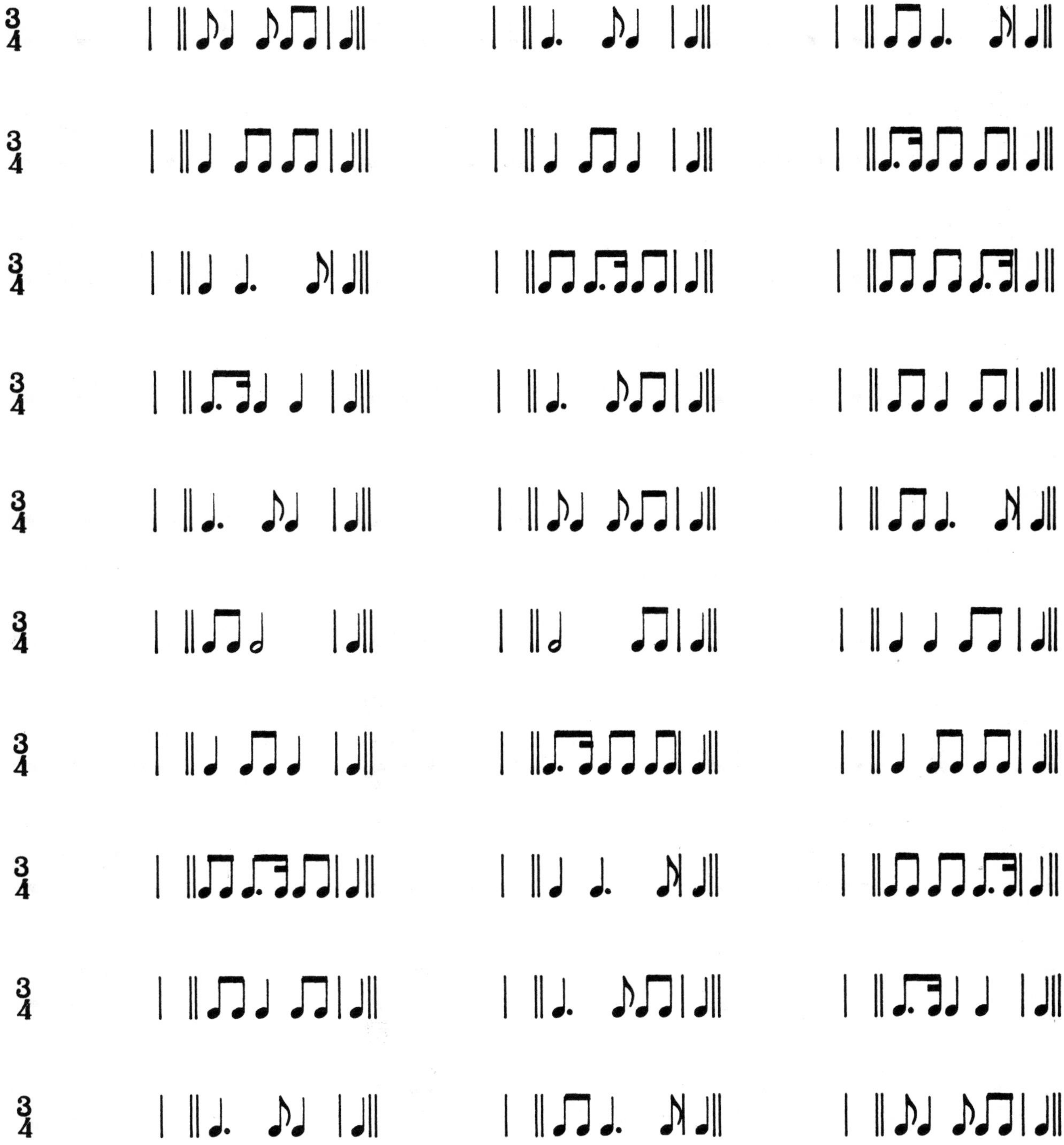

B4-1   Rhythmic dictation
(Copy 3)

Shield the answer. Listen to the melody and write the rhythm; then check your response. Circle incorrect responses. Stop the tape between frames. Goal: No more than eight incorrect frames.

128

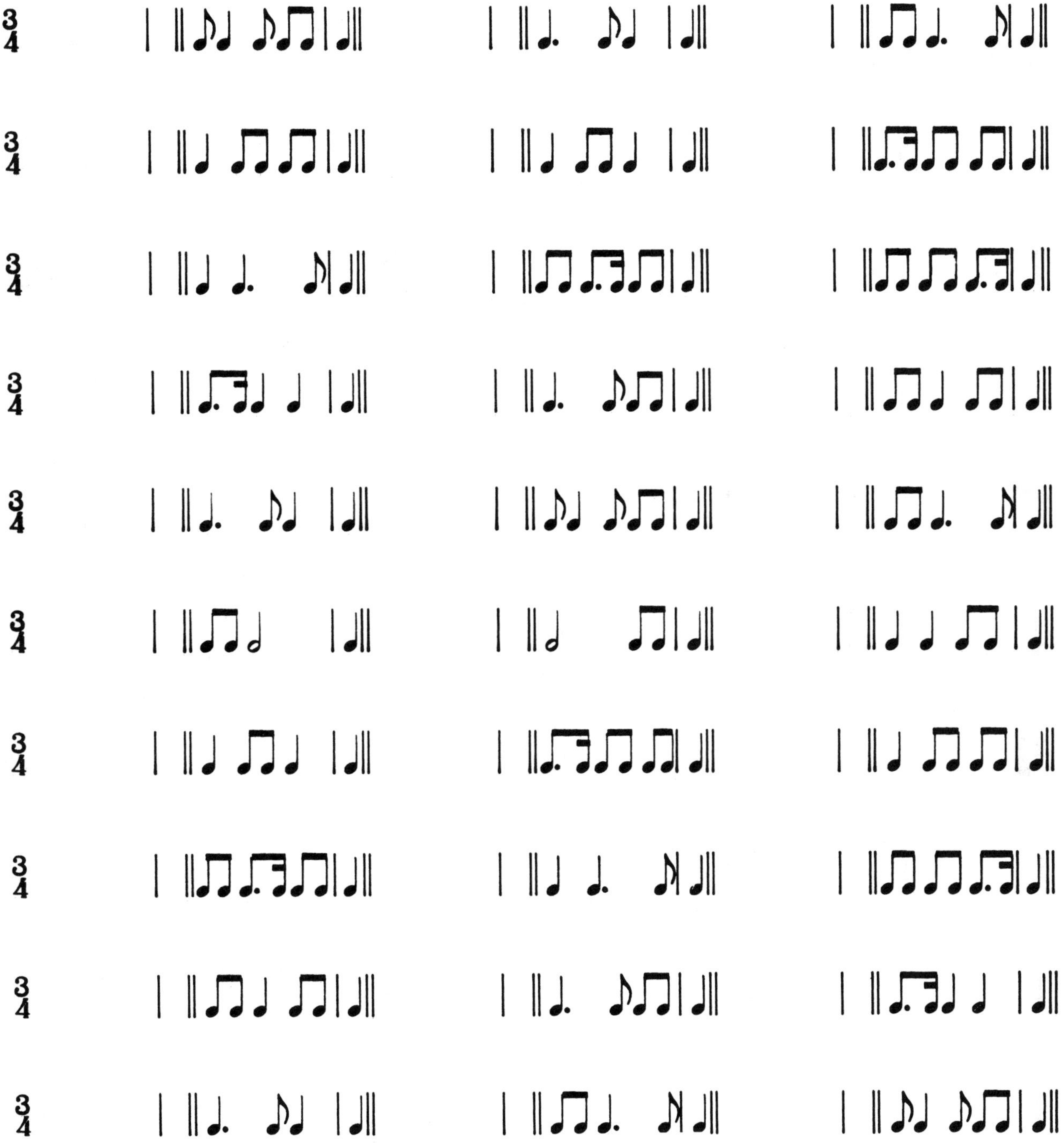

Rhythmic dictation

Shield the answer. Listen to the melody and write the rhythm; then check your response. Circle incorrect responses. Stop the tape between frames. Goal: No more than eight incorrect frames.

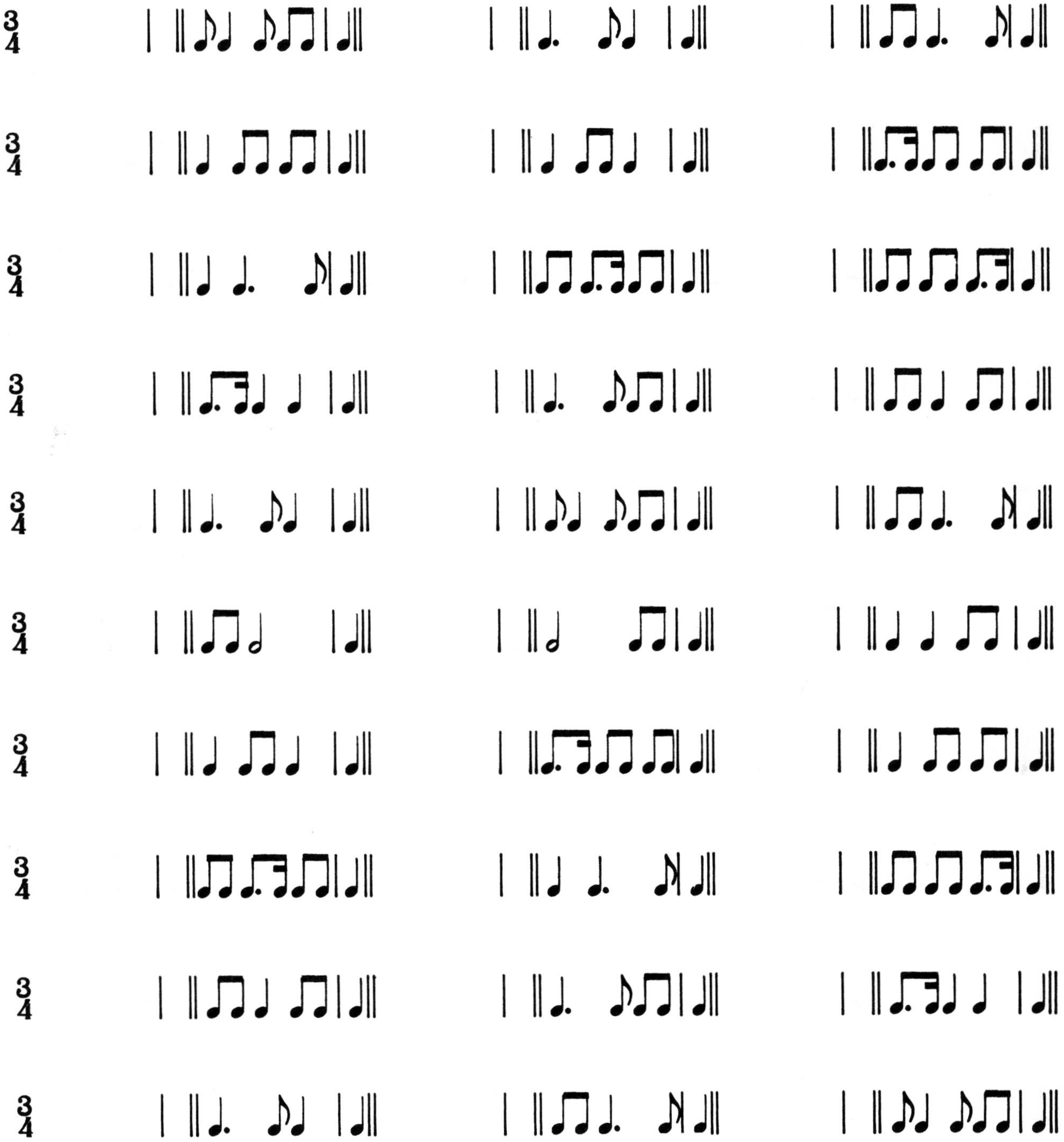

B4-1

(Copy 5)

Rhythmic dictation

Shield the answer. Listen to the melody and write the rhythm; then check your response. Circle incorrect responses. Stop the tape between frames. Goal: No more than eight incorrect frames.

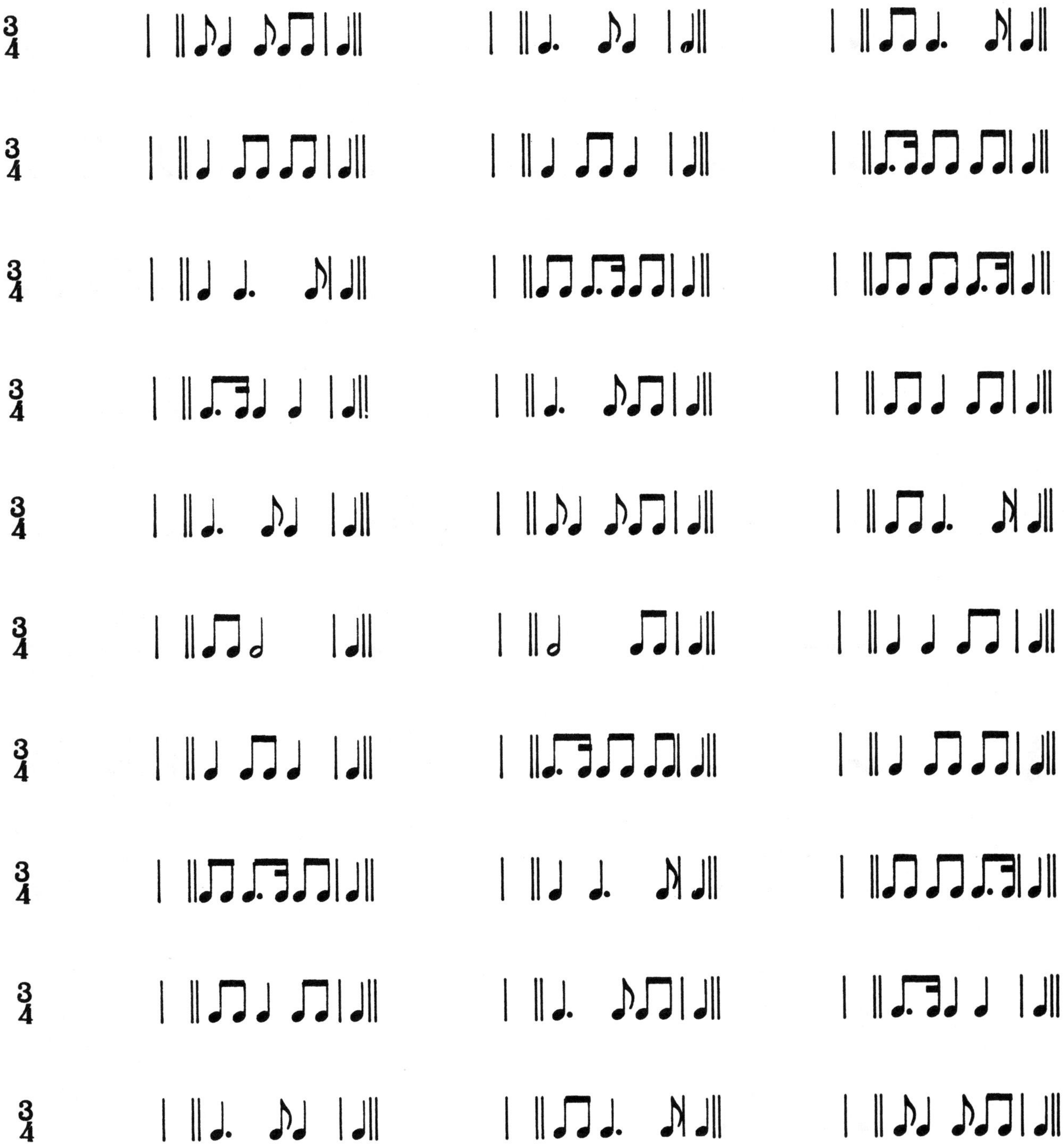

Rhythmic dictation

Shield the answer. Listen to the melody and write the rhythm; then check your response. Circle incorrect responses. Stop the tape between frames. Goal: No more than eight incorrect frames.

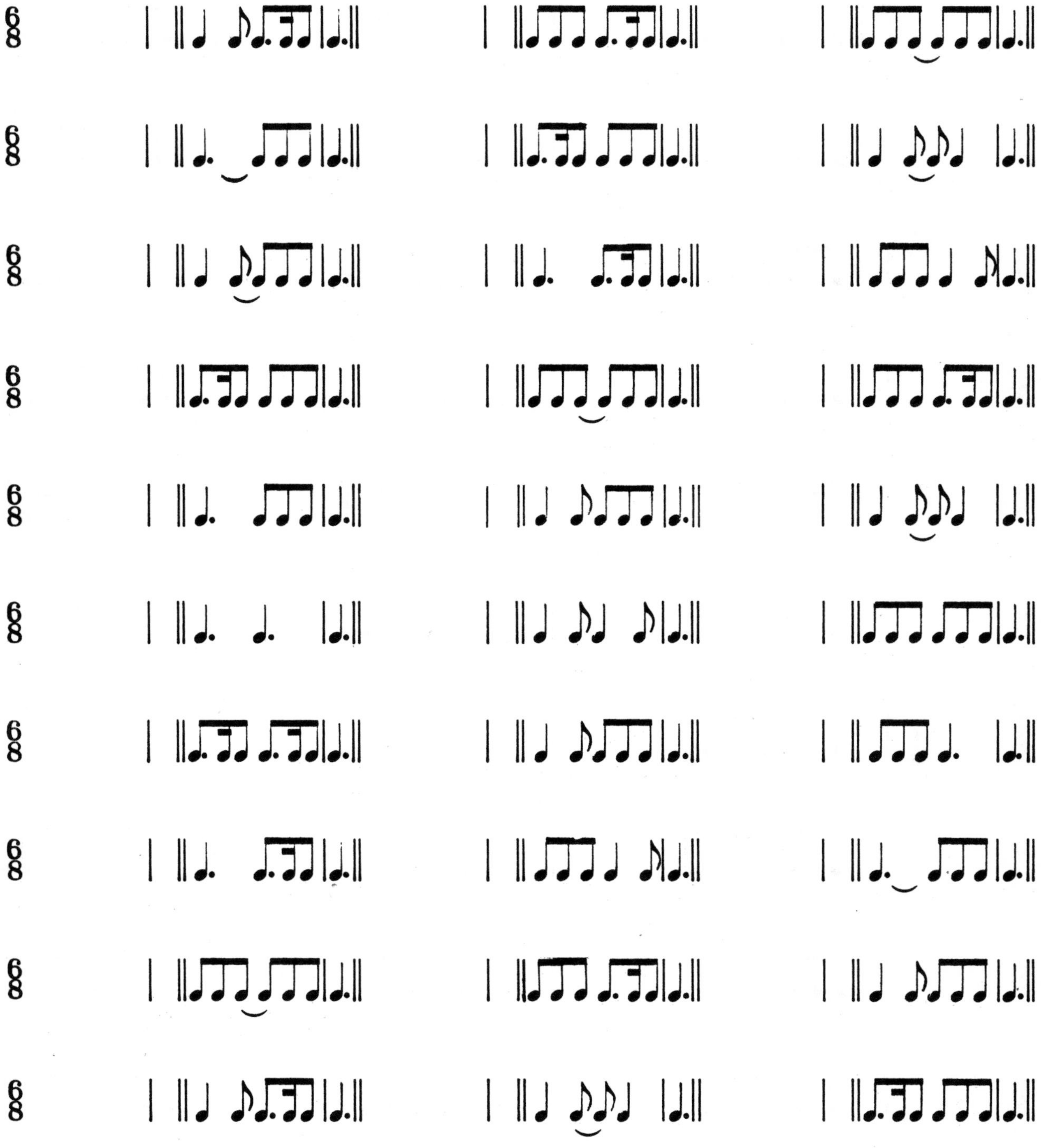

Rhythmic dictation

(Copy 2)

Shield the answer. Listen to the melody and write the rhythm; then check your response. Circle incorrect responses. Stop the tape between frames. Goal: No more than eight incorrect frames.

137

B4-2 Rhythmic dictation
(Copy 3)

Shield the answer. Listen to the melody and write the rhythm; then check your response. Circle incorrect responses. Stop the tape between frames. Goal: No more than eight incorrect frames.

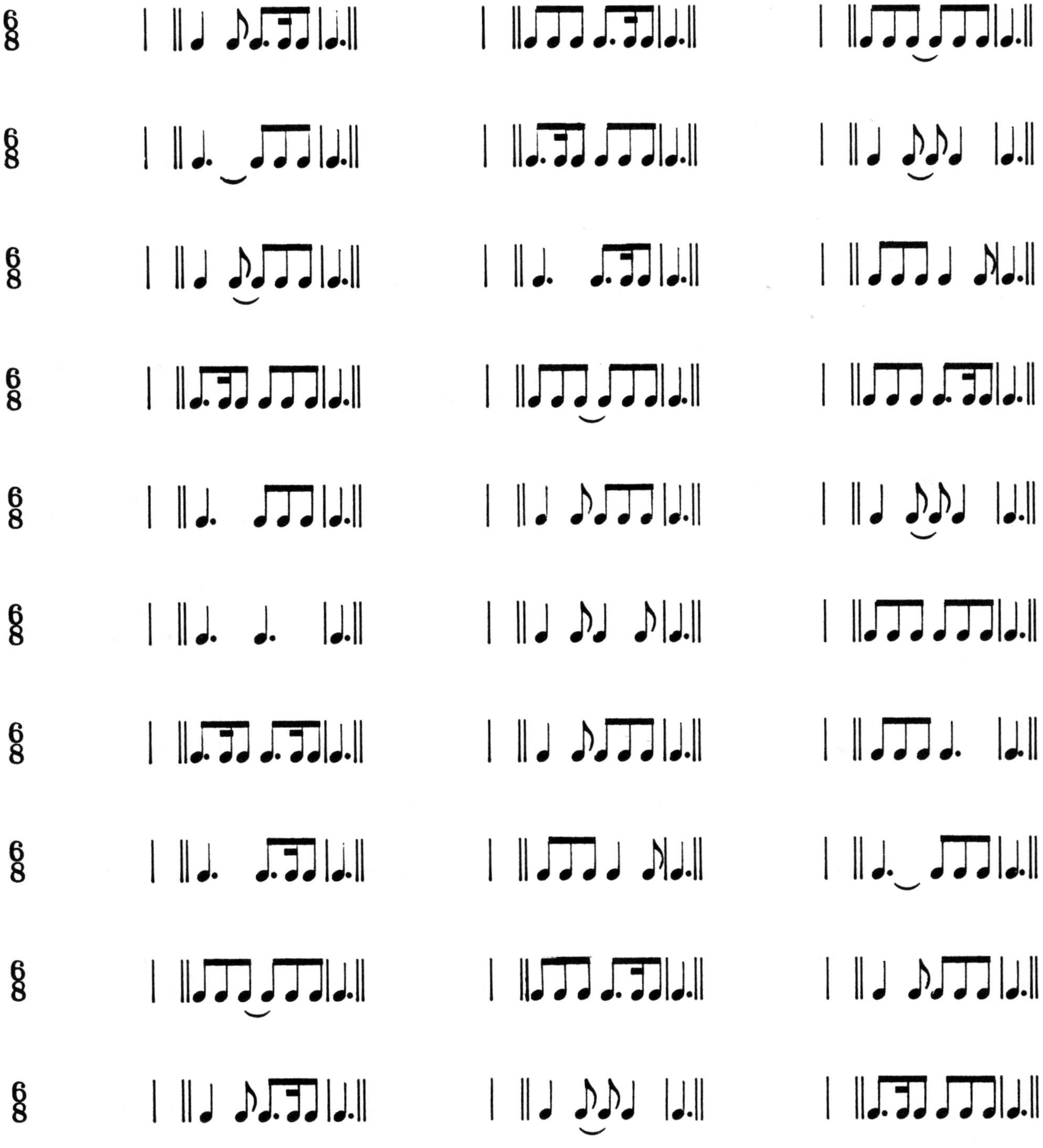

B4-2   Rhythmic dictation
(Copy 4)

Shield the answer. Listen to the melody and write the rhythm; then check your response. Circle incorrect responses. Stop the tape between frames. Goal: No more than eight incorrect frames.

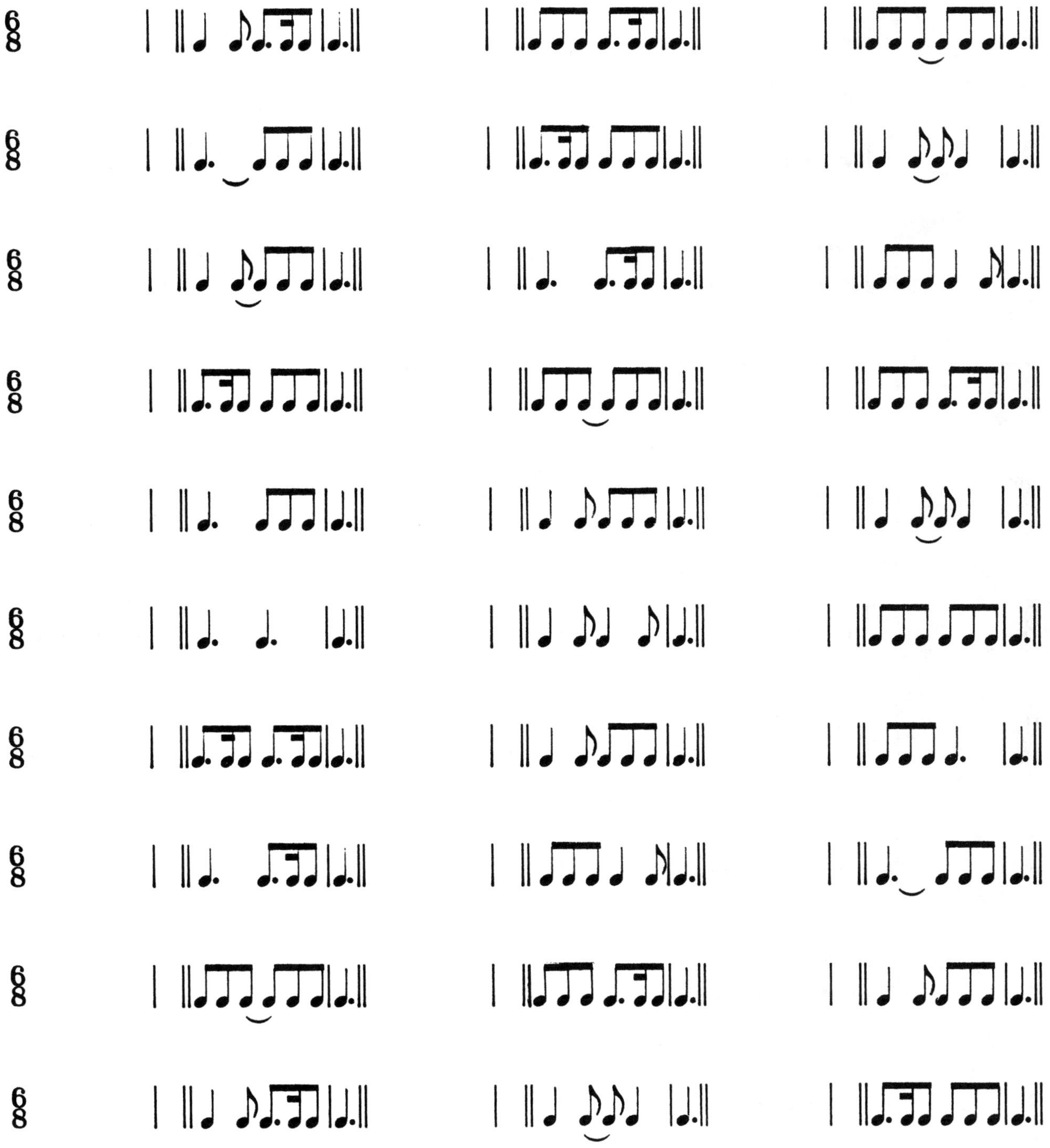

Rhythmic dictation

Shield the answer. Listen to the melody and write the rhythm; then check your response. Circle incorrect responses. Stop the tape between frames. Goal: No more than eight incorrect frames.

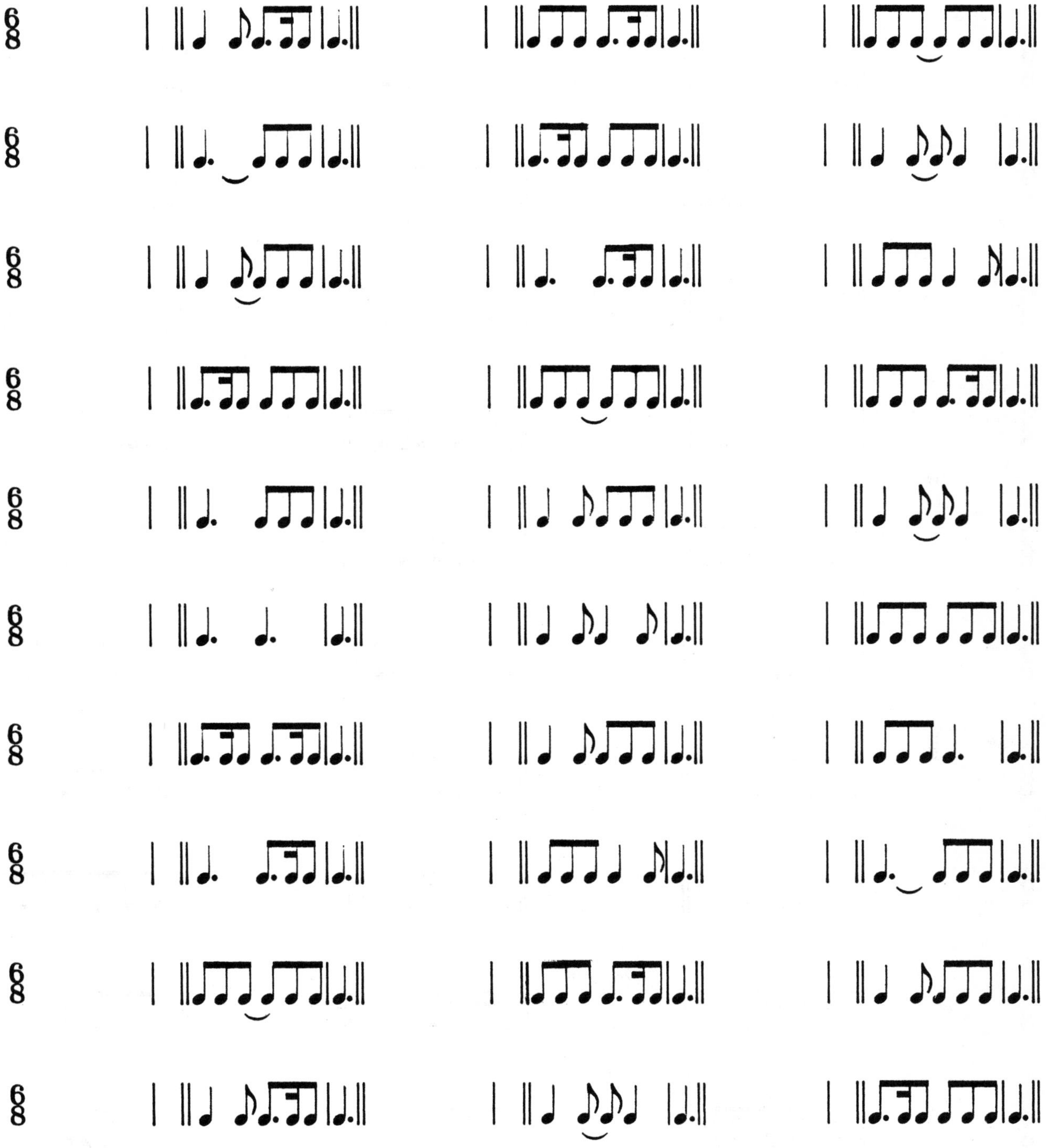

Rhythmic dictation

Shield the answer. Listen to the melody and write the rhythm; then check your response. Circle incorrect responses. Stop the tape between frames. Goal: No more than eight incorrect frames.

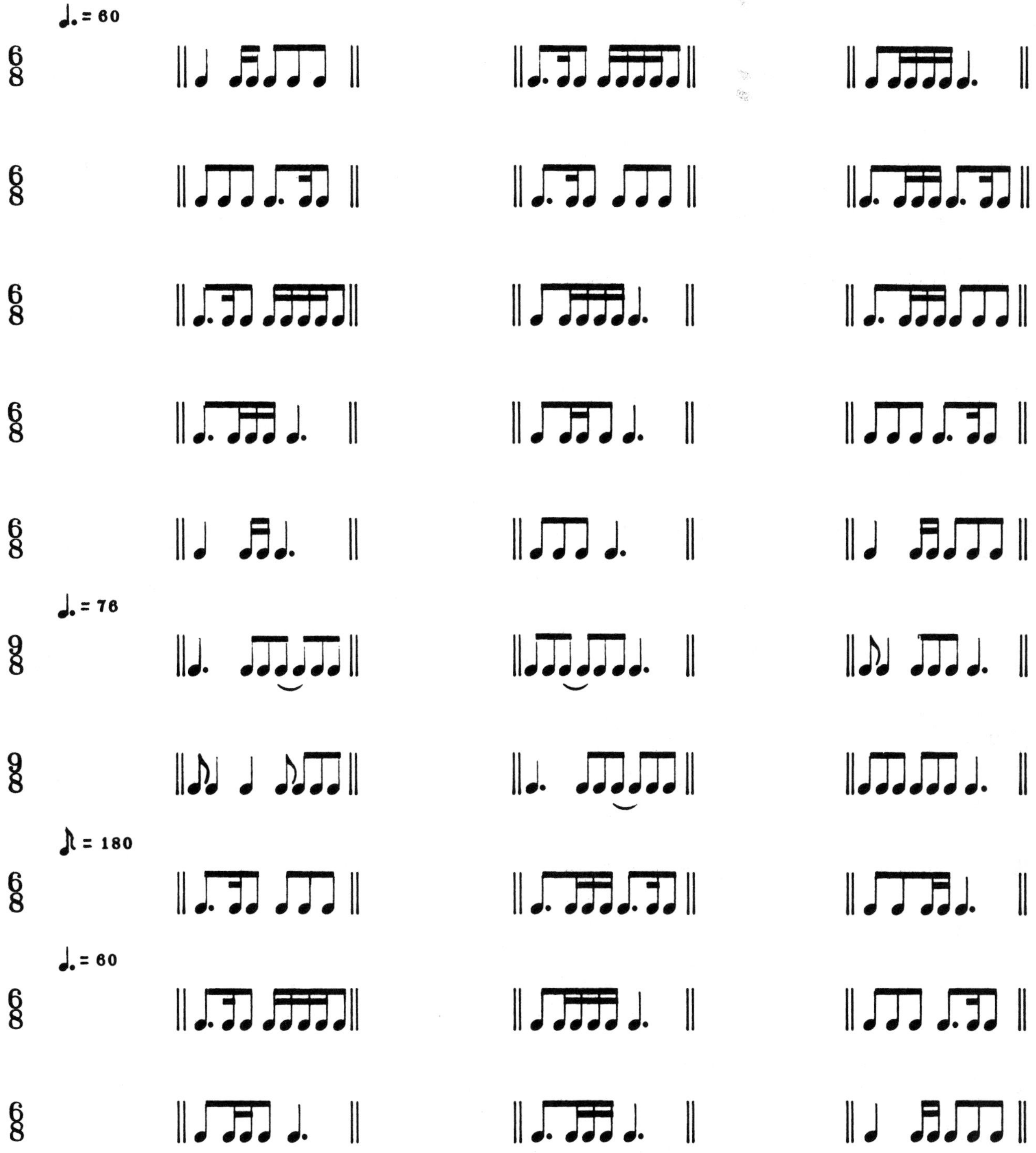
= 60
6 8
6 8
6 8
6 8
6 8
= 76
9 8
9 8
= 180
6 8
= 60
6 8
6 8

B4-3

(Copy 2)

Rhythmic dictation

Shield the answer. Listen to the melody and write the rhythm; then check your response. Circle incorrect responses. Stop the tape between frames. Goal: No more than eight incorrect frames.

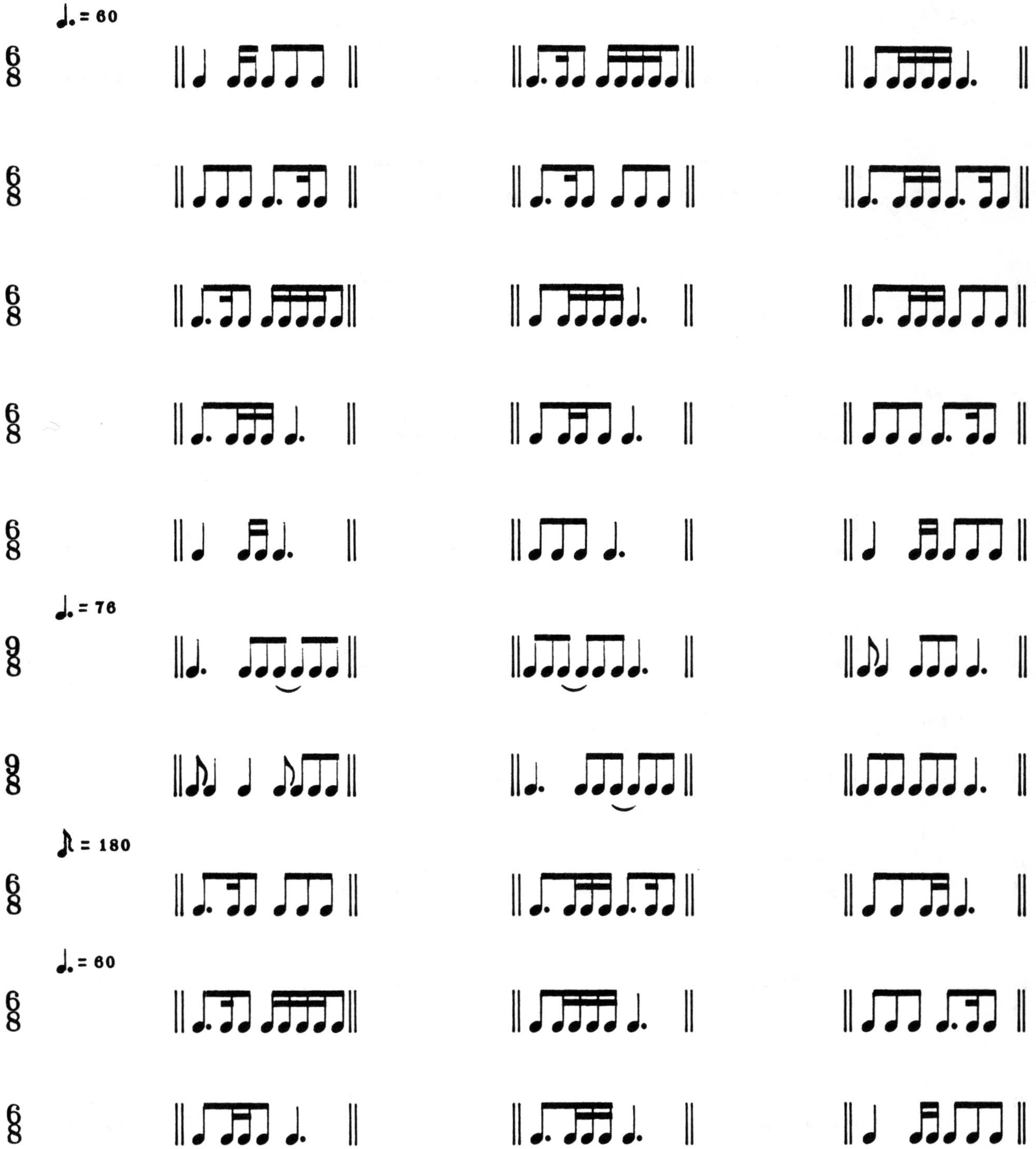
= 60
= 76
= 180
= 60

B4-3
(Copy 3)

Rhythmic dictation

Shield the answer. Listen to the melody and write the rhythm; then check your response. Circle incorrect responses. Stop the tape between frames. Goal: No more than eight incorrect frames.

148

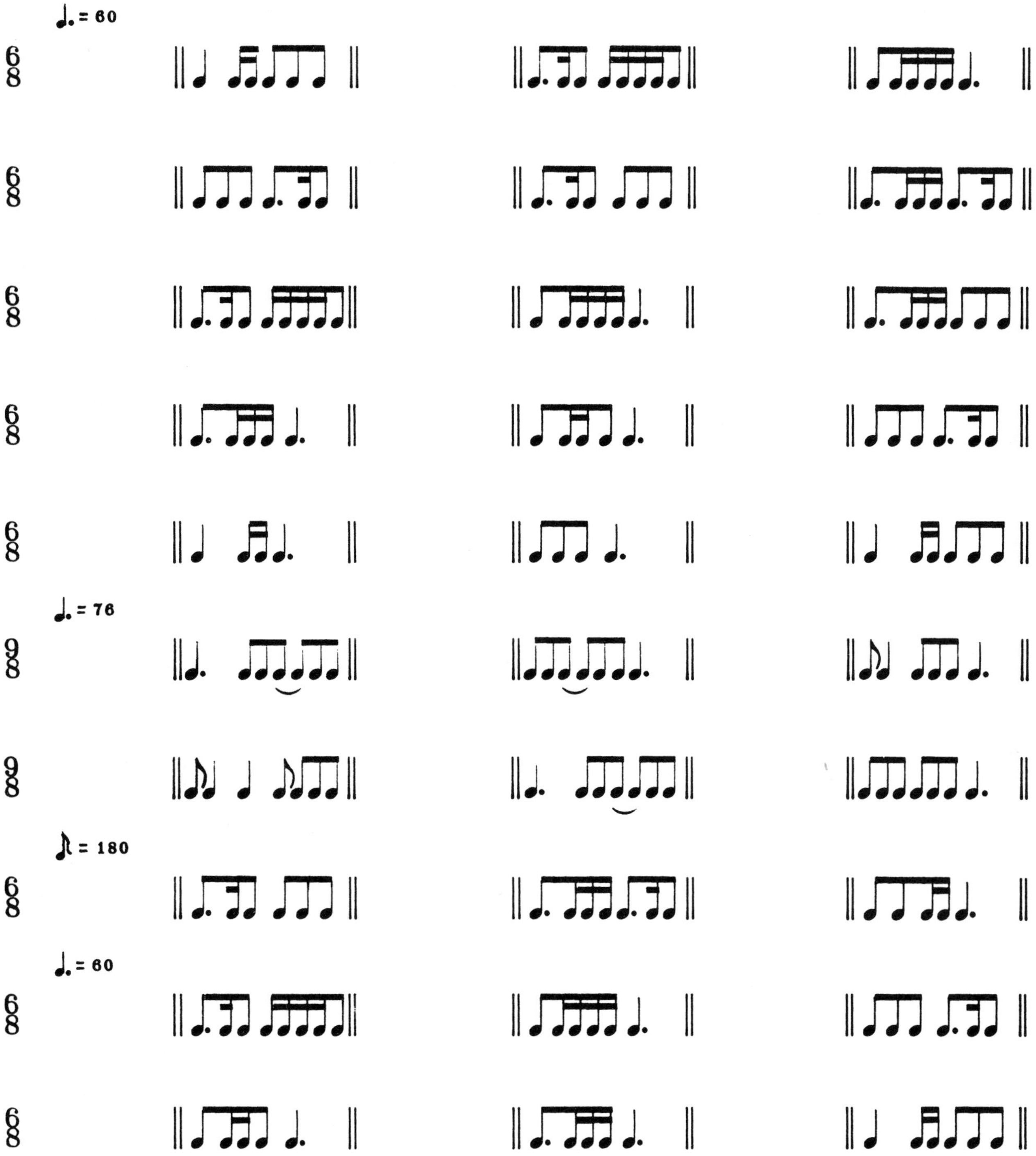
= 60
= 76
= 180
= 60

B4-3 Rhythmic dictation
(Copy 4)

Shield the answer. Listen to the melody and write the rhythm; then check your response. Circle incorrect responses. Stop the tape between frames. Goal: No more than eight incorrect frames.

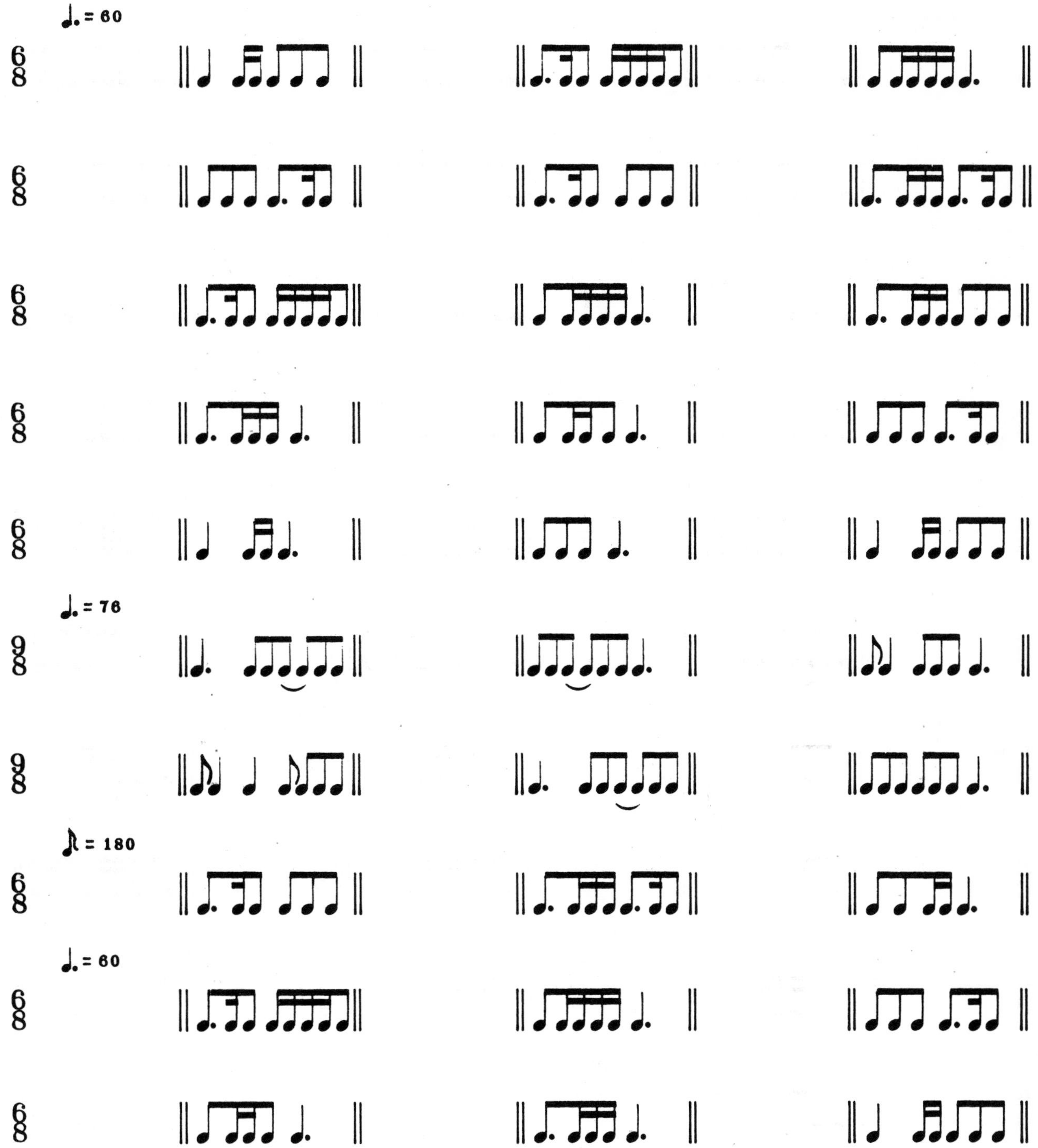
= 60
= 76
= 180
= 60

Rhythmic dictation

Shield the answer. Listen to the melody and write the rhythm; then check your response. Circle incorrect responses. Stop the tape between frames. Goal: No more than eight incorrect frames.

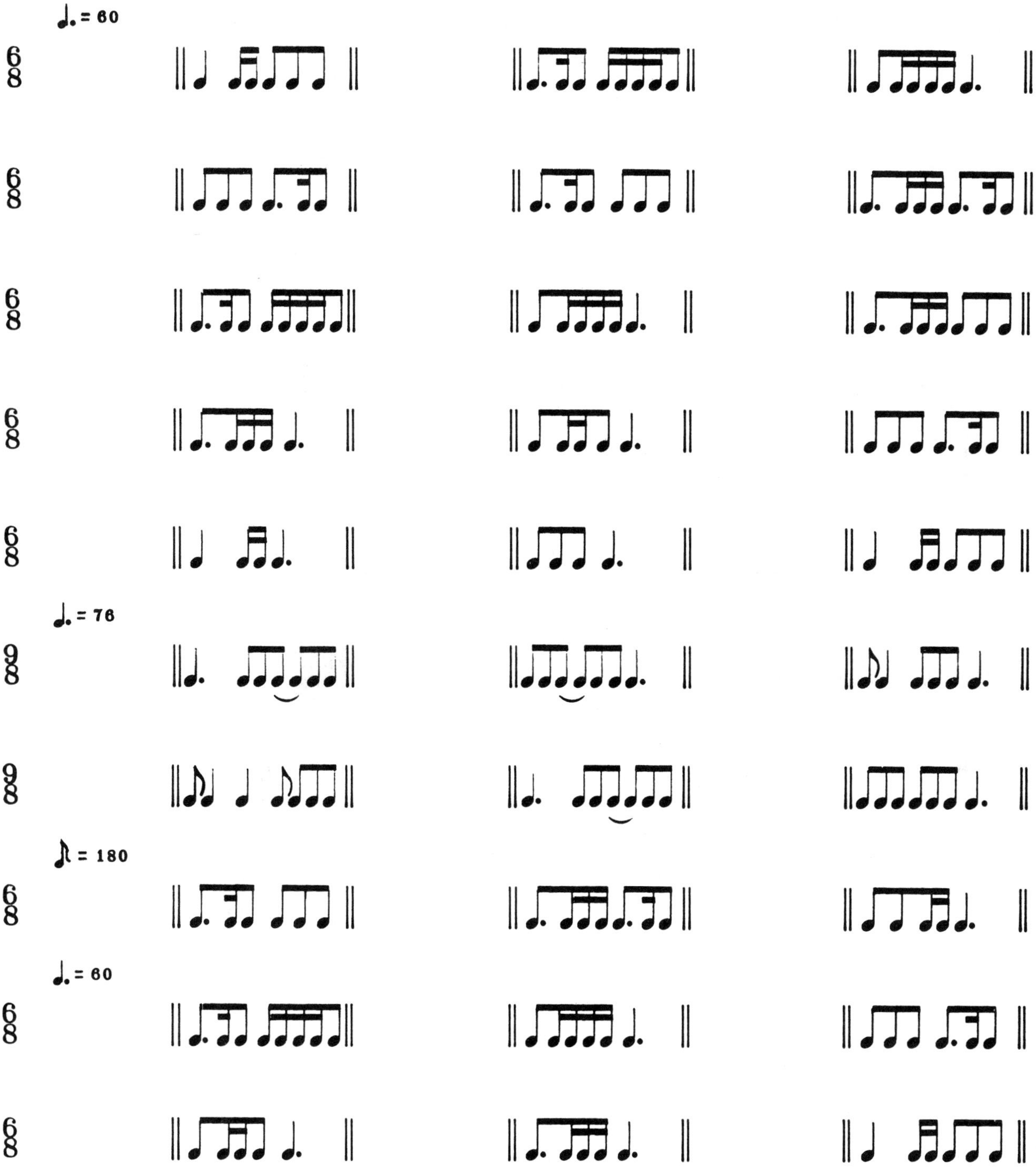
= 60
6/8
6/8
6/8
6/8
6/8
= 76
9/8
9/8
= 180
6/8
= 60
6/8
6/8

B4-4

(Copy 1)

Rhythmic dictation

Shield the answer. Listen to the melody and write the rhythm; then check your response. Circle incorrect responses. Stop the tape between frames. Goal: No more than eight incorrect frames. After you have done this lesson, take Test B4.

155

B4-4　Rhythmic dictation
(Copy 2)

Shield the answer. Listen to the melody and write the rhythm; then check your response. Circle incorrect responses. Stop the tape between frames. Goal: No more than eight incorrect frames. After you have done this lesson, take Test B4.

157

B4-4 Rhythmic dictation
(Copy 3)

Shield the answer. Listen to the melody and·write the rhythm; then check your response. Circle incorrect responses. Stop the tape between frames. Goal: No more than eight incorrect frames. After you have done this lesson, take Test B4.

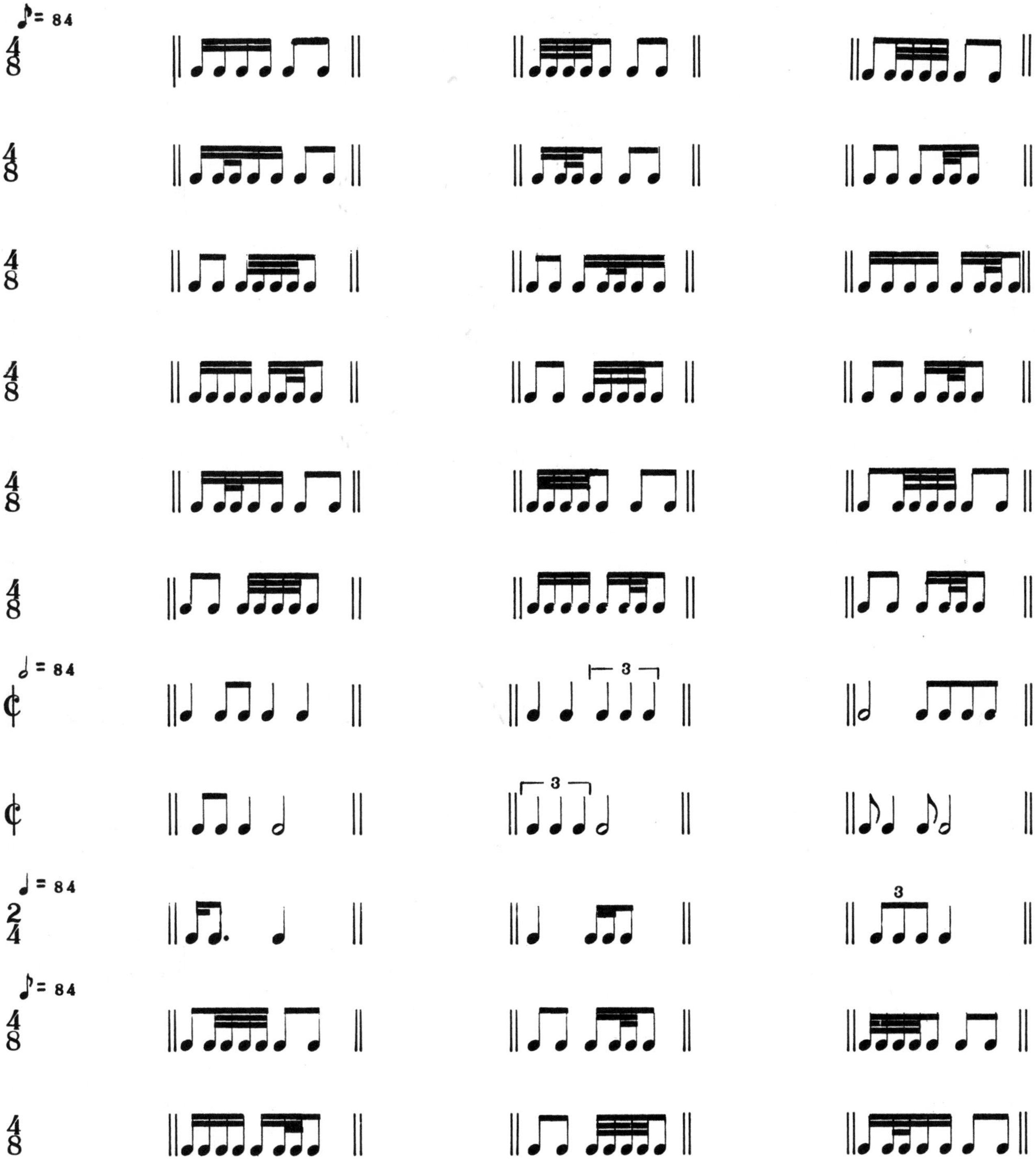
= 84
= 84
= 84
= 84

B4-4　Rhythmic dictation
(Copy 4)

Shield the answer. Listen to the melody and write the rhythm; then check your response. Circle incorrect responses. Stop the tape between frames. Goal: No more than eight incorrect frames. After you have done this lesson, take Test B4.

160

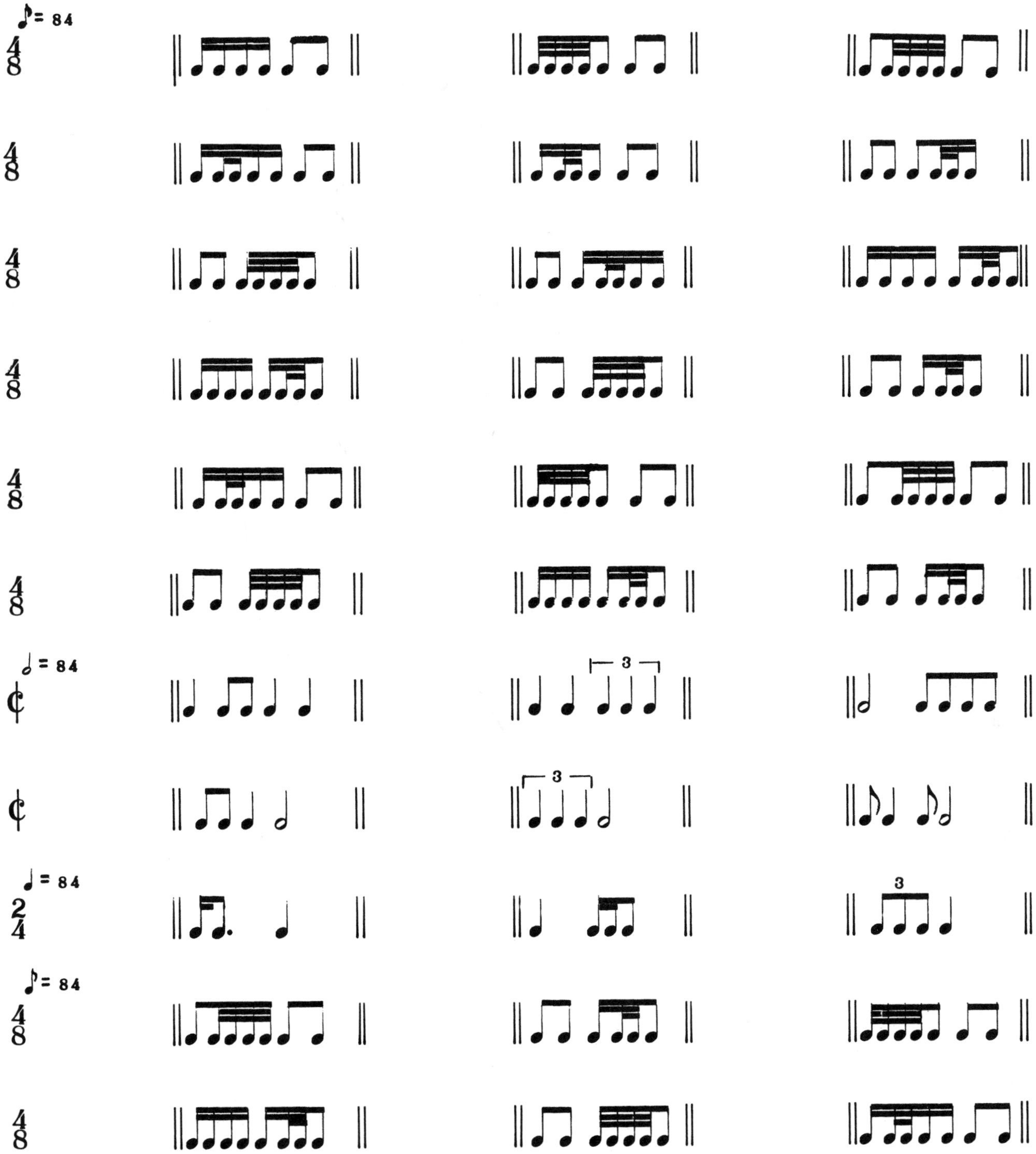

B4-4
(Copy 5)

Rhythmic dictation

Shield the answer. Listen to the melody and write the rhythm; then check your response. Circle incorrect responses. Stop the tape between frames. Goal: No more than eight incorrect frames. After you have done this lesson, take Test B4.

162

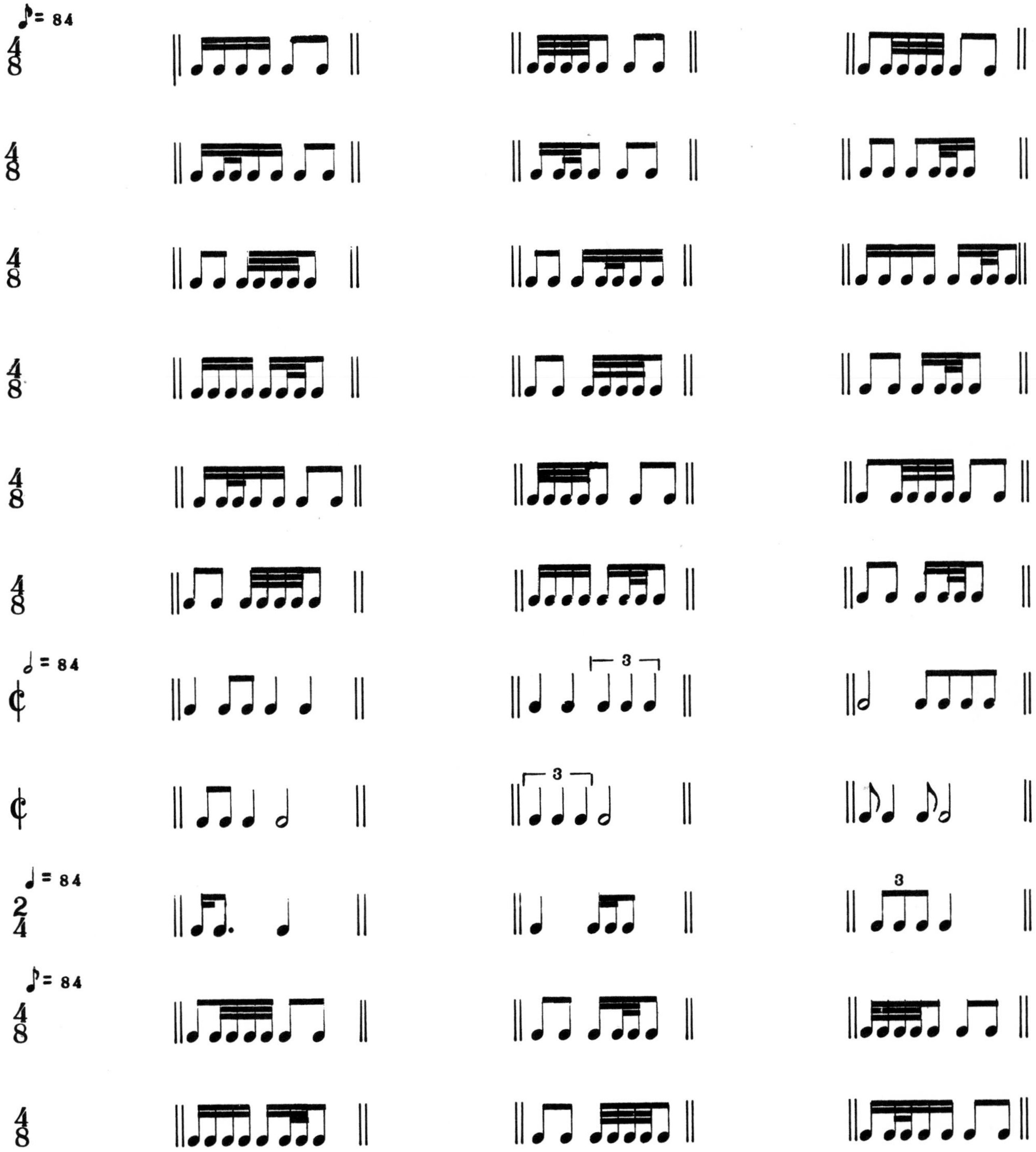

Intermediate Sightsinging— Melody and Rhythm

In this series there are eight *sightsinging lessons.* The procedure for the lessons in this series is the same as for Series B2: a printed worksheet and a tape recording are provided for each lesson. The frames on the worksheet are separated by double bar lines. You will hear the starting note only for the first frame. For all other frames you must find the first note from the preceding frame. To do each frame, sing the printed melody in time with the metronome. You will then hear the melody correctly performed. Whenever you have not sung a melody correctly, make a tally mark on a piece of paper. Your goal is to have no more than eight incorrect frames in an entire lesson. When you have reached this goal, go on to the next lesson. If you have more than eight incorrect frames, repeat the lesson until you reach the goal or until you have done the lesson five times, at which point you should go on to the next lesson regardless of the number of errors.

When you have done this series, take Test B5.

B5-1   Sightsinging

Sing each frame in time with the metronome and compare your response with the melody you then hear. The starting tone is given for the first frame only. Tally errors on a separate sheet of paper. Goal: No more than eight incorrect frames.

167

B5-2   Sightsinging

Sing each frame in time with the metronome and compare your response with the melody you then hear. The starting tone is given for the first frame only. Tally errors on a separate sheet of paper. Goal: No more than eight incorrect frames.

B5-3 Sightsinging

Sing each frame in time with the metronome and compare your response with the melody you then hear. The starting tone is given for the first frame only. Tally errors on a separate sheet of paper. Goal: No more than eight incorrect frames.

171

B5-4 Sightsinging

Sing each frame in time with the metronome and compare your response with the melody you then hear. The starting tone is given for the first frame only. Tally errors on a separate sheet of paper. Goal: No more than eight incorrect frames.

172

B5-5 Sightsinging

Sing each frame in time with the metronome and compare your response with the melody you then hear. The starting tone is given for the first frame only. Tally errors on a separate sheet of paper. Goal: No more than eight incorrect frames.

B5-6 Sightsinging

Sing each frame in time with the metronome and compare your response with the melody you then hear. The starting tone is given for the first frame only. Tally errors on a separate sheet of paper. Goal: No more than eight incorrect frames.

177

B5-7 Sightsinging

Sing each frame in time with the metronome and compare your response with the melody you then hear. The starting tone is given for the first frame only. Tally errors on a separate sheet of paper. Goal: No more than eight incorrect frames.

178

179

B5-8 Sightsinging

*Sing each frame in time with the metronome and compare your response with the melody you then
hear. The starting tone is given for the first frame only. Tally errors on a separate piece of paper. Goal:
No more than eight incorrect frames. After you have done this lesson, take Test B5.*

180

181

Intermediate Dictation— Melody and Rhythm

SERIES B6

In this series, there are four *melodic dictation lessons*. The procedure for the lessons in this series is the same as for Series B3: a printed worksheet and a tape recording are provided for each lesson. To do each frame, start by shielding the printed answer. When you have heard the melody, stop the tape and notate it. Then slide the shield to the right and compare your response with the printed answer. Circle each frame in which your response is not entirely correct. Your goal is to complete each lesson with no more than eight incorrect frames. When you have reached this goal, go on to the next lesson. If you have more than eight incorrect frames, repeat the lesson until you reach the goal or until you have done the lesson five times, at which point you should go on to the next lesson regardless of the number of errors.

When you have done this series, take Test B6.

B6-1

(Copy 1)

Melodic dictation

Shield the answer. Listen to the melody and notate it; then check your response. Circle incorrect responses. Stop the tape between frames. Goal: No more than eight incorrect frames.

185

186

B6-1

(Copy 2)

Melodic dictation

Shield the answer. Listen to the melody and notate it; then check your response. Circle incorrect responses. Stop the tape between frames. Goal: No more than eight incorrect frames.

188

189

B6-1 Melodic dictation

(Copy 3)

Shield the answer. Listen to the melody and notate it; then check your response. Circle incorrect responses. Stop the tape between frames. Goal: No more than eight incorrect frames.

190

191

192

Melodic dictation

Shield the answer. Listen to the melody and notate it; then check your response. Circle incorrect responses. Stop the tape between frames. Goal: No more than eight incorrect frames.

194

B6-1

(Copy 5)

Melodic dictation

Shield the answer. Listen to the melody and notate it; then check your response. Circle incorrect responses. Stop the tape between frames. Goal: No more than eight incorrect frames.

197

198

B6-2

(Copy 1)

Melodic dictation

Shield the answer. Listen to the melody and notate it; then check your response. Circle incorrect responses. Stop the tape between frames. Goal: No more than eight incorrect frames.

200

201

B6-2 Melodic dictation
(Copy 2)

Shield the answer. Listen to the melody and notate it; then check your response. Circle incorrect responses. Stop the tape between frames. Goal: No more than eight incorrect frames.

203

204

B6-2 Melodic dictation

(Copy 3)

Shield the answer. Listen to the melody and notate it; then check your response. Circle incorrect responses. Stop the tape between frames. Goal: No more than eight incorrect frames.

206

207

B6-2
(Copy 4)

Melodic dictation

Shield the answer. Listen to the melody and notate it; then check your response. Circle incorrect responses. Stop the tape between frames. Goal: No more than eight incorrect frames.

209

210

B6-2 Melodic dictation

(Copy 5)

Shield the answer. Listen to the melody and notate it; then check your response. Circle incorrect responses. Stop the tape between frames. Goal: No more than eight incorrect frames.

212

213

B6-3
(Copy 1)

Melodic dictation

Shield the answer. Listen to the melody and notate it; then check your response. Circle incorrect responses. Stop the tape between frames. Goal: No more than eight incorrect frames.

215

216

B6-3

(Copy 2)

Melodic dictation

Shield the answer. Listen to the melody and notate it; then check your response. Circle incorrect responses. Stop the tape between frames. Goal: No more than eight incorrect frames.

217

218

219

B6-3

(Copy 3)

Melodic dictation

Shield the answer. Listen to the melody and notate it; then check your response. Circle incorrect responses. Stop the tape between frames. Goal: No more than eight incorrect frames.

221

222

B6-3 Melodic dictation
(Copy 4)

Shield the answer. Listen to the melody and notate it; then check your response. Circle incorrect responses. Stop the tape between frames. Goal: No more than eight incorrect frames.

223

B6-3
(Copy 5)

Melodic dictation

Shield the answer. Listen to the melody and notate it; then check your response. Circle incorrect responses. Stop the tape between frames. Goal: No more than eight incorrect frames.

227

228

B6-4

(Copy 1)

Melodic dictation

Shield the answer. Listen to the melody and notate it; then check your response. Circle incorrect responses. Stop the tape between frames. Goal: No more than eight incorrect frames. After you have done this lesson, take Test B6.

230

231

B6-4　Melodic dictation
(Copy 2)

Shield the answer. Listen to the melody and notate it; then check your response. Circle incorrect responses. Stop the tape between frames. Goal: No more than eight incorrect frames. After you have done this lesson, take Test B6.

233

234

B6-4 Melodic dictation

Shield the answer. Listen to the melody and notate it; then check your response. Circle incorrect responses. Stop the tape between frames. Goal: No more than eight incorrect frames. After you have done this lesson, take Test B6.

235

236

237

B6-4

(Copy 4)

Melodic dictation

Shield the answer. Listen to the melody and notate it; then check your response. Circle incorrect responses. Stop the tape between frames. Goal: No more than eight incorrect frames. After you have done this lesson. take Test B6.

239

240

B6-4
(Copy 5)

Melodic dictation

Shield the answer. Listen to the melody and notate it; then check your response. Circle incorrect responses. Stop the tape between frames. Goal: No more than eight incorrect frames. After you have done this lesson, take Test B6.

242

243

Intermediate Sightsinging— Complete Phrases

In this series, there are three lessons in *sightsinging complete phrases*. The purpose of the lessons in sightsinging complete phrases is to develop your ability to sing longer melodies. A worksheet and a tape recording are provided for each lesson. Each frame on the worksheet takes one complete line. To do each frame, start by listening to the tape recording. You will hear a metronome clicking at the tempo in which you should sing and the pitch of the first note of the frame. Observe the metronome marking on the worksheet to determine the note value which receives one beat of the metronome. Stop the tape after hearing the initial material and sing the melody. Then, starting the tape, you will hear the melody correctly performed and can judge if your response was correct. Examine the melody before singing it to determine the key and the degree of the key on which the melody begins. For those melodies which do not begin on the tonic, you may find it helpful to sing scalewise from the starting note to the tonic in order to establish the key. Each lesson in this series should be done only once in preparation for the test. The test itself will serve to measure your achievement. If you wish to raise your test score, you should do each lesson once more and then take the test again.

When you have done this series, take Test B7.

B7-1 Sightsinging complete phrases

Listen to the starting tone and the metronome. Stop the tape and sing the phrase. Then start the tape and compare your response. Do this lesson once in preparation for the test.

246

B7-2 Sightsinging complete phrases

Listen to the starting tone and the metronome. Stop the tape and sing the phrase. Then start the tape and compare your response. Do this lesson once in preparation for the test.

249

B7-3   Sightsinging complete phrases

Listen to the starting tone and the metronome. Stop the tape and sing the phrase. Then start the tape and compare your response. Do this lesson once in preparation for the test. After you have done this lesson, take Test B7.

251

Dictation—Bar Lines and Meter **SERIES B8**

In this series there are lessons of two kinds: *bar line placement,* and *rhythmic dictation of complete phrases.* One of the problems in writing music from dictation is the determination of meter and the place of bar lines. These are the chief problems in this series. The bar line in music usually tells two things: the length of the measure, and the position of the first beat of each measure.

The first beat in the measure, often called the downbeat, is usually the strongest or most emphasized beat. There are several characteristics in music which can help make a beat sound like a downbeat. A beat tends to sound like a downbeat:

1. if it is louder, or accented.
2. if the note beginning on this beat is longer than notes around it.
3. if it occupies the same position in a repeated rhythmic pattern as previous downbeats.
4. if there is a chord change at this point.

It is possible that these indications will be contradictory, and that some will be more important than others. Generally, when the music contains chords, the chord change is likely to indicate the downbeat even where the other characteristics are contradictory. Where the music is not harmonized or where there are not important chord changes, strong regular accents are usually more important than long notes in determining the downbeat.

In the example below, the first downbeat is clearly on the first note, which is accented.

In the next example, assuming there are no strong accents, the first downbeat is indicated to be on the third note because it is longer than the notes around it.

Once the first downbeat is determined, the length of measure can be determined either by listening for other accented or long notes, or by noting the length of repeated rhythmic patterns. In both examples above, the length of the repeated pattern makes it clear that there is a downbeat every third quarter note value, and thus the most probable meter is 3/4.

Of course, it is usually not necessary to analyze in this way to find the downbeat. Instead the above characteristics simply make certain beats sound like downbeats, and, with very little practice, it is possible to detect the position of downbeats without being particularly aware of what makes them sound this way.

When you have done this series, take Test B8 which is a test in rhythmic dictation of complete phrases. The test does not include a section on bar line placement. While your achievement in this skill is not tested, it will help you in rhythmic dictation of complete phrases which is tested.

Lessons **B8-1, B8-2, B8-3** and **B8-4**

These are lessons in bar line placement. A worksheet and a tape recording are provided for each lesson. In each frame on the worksheet the note values for a melody are written without bar lines. You are to place the bar lines in the appropriate places after you have heard the melody. The answer printed below the sequence of notes shows the proper positions of the bar lines. To do each frame, start by shielding the answer. Follow the printed notes while listening to the melody and try to judge or feel where the downbeats are. Draw a bar line before each downbeat, then uncover the answer and check your response. You may stop the tape recording between frames. Circle each frame in which your response is incorrect. Your goal is to complete each lesson with no more than five incorrect frames. When you done this, go on to the next lesson. If you have more than five incorrect frames, repeat the lesson until you reach the goal or until you have done the lesson five times, at which point you should go on to the next lesson regardless of the number of errors.

In these lessons, various characteristics are used to indicate downbeat. In lessons B8-1, B8-2, and B8-3, which have melodies that are not harmonized, you may expect the first downbeat to be indicated either by a strong accent or by a note longer than the others around it. In lesson B8-4, which has harmonized melodies, you may expect chord changes at the downbeats.

B8-1 Bar line placement
(Copy 1)

Shield the answer below the notes. Listen to the melody and show where the bar lines should appear; then check your response. Stop the tape between frames. Goal: No more than five incorrect frames.

The following rhythms are in 3/4 meter.

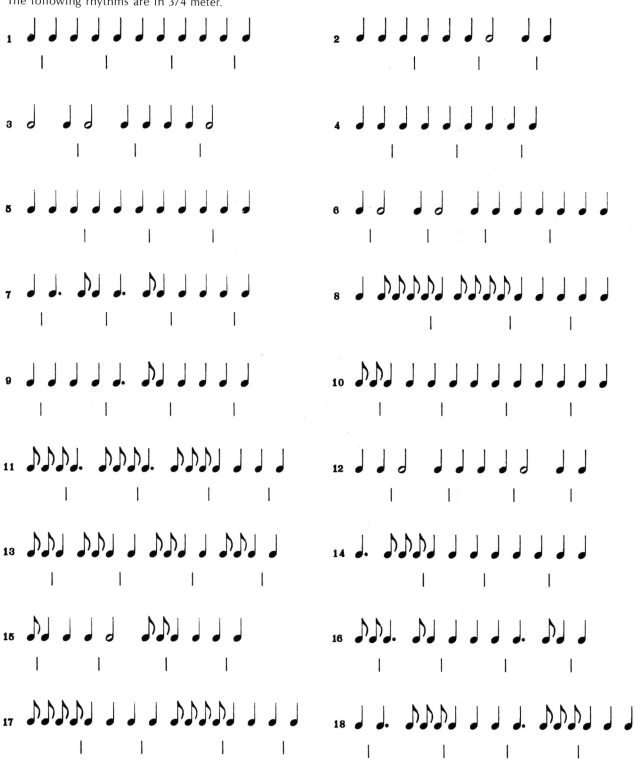

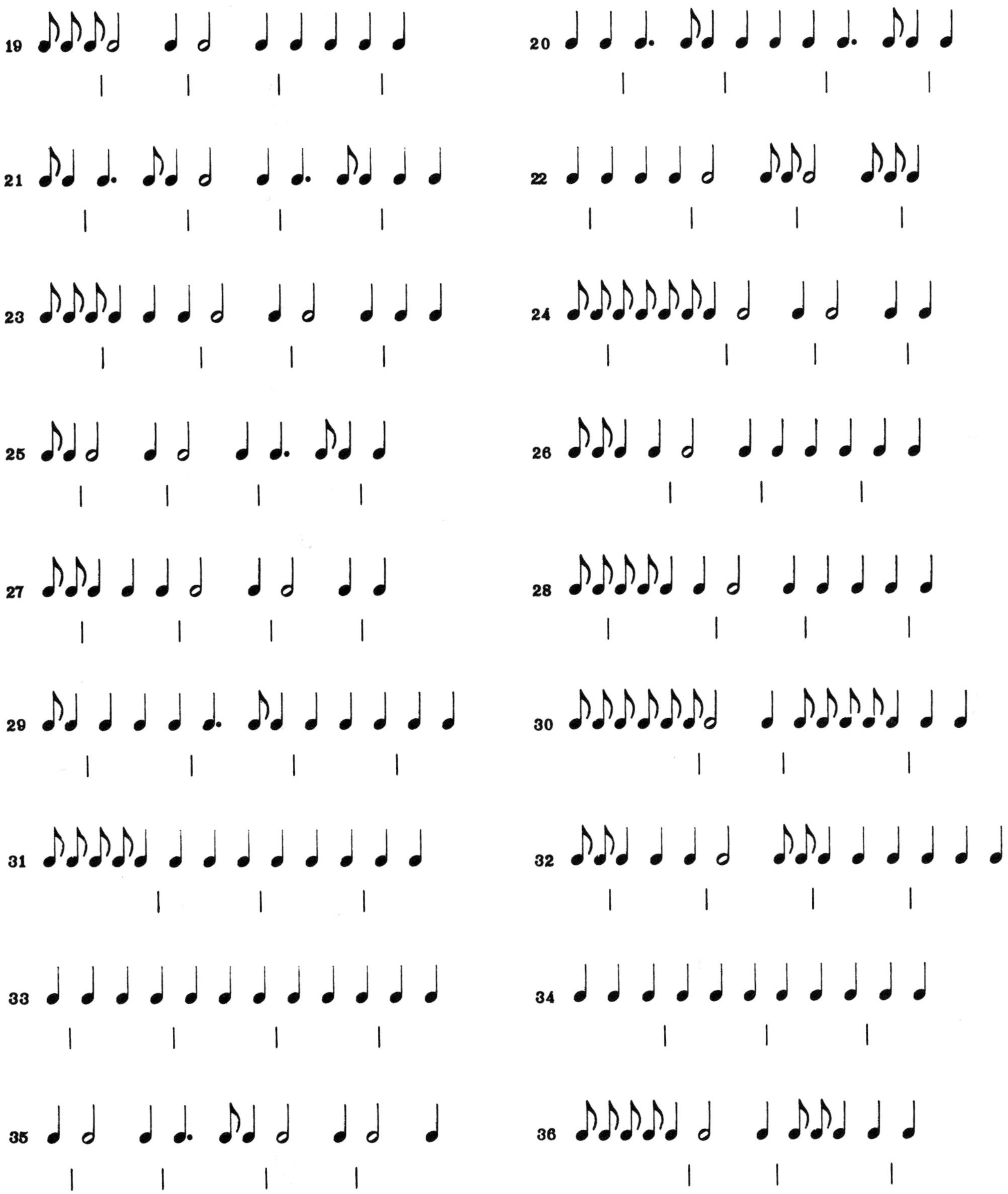
19
20
21
22
23
24
25
26
27
28
29
30
31
32
33
34
35
36

B8-1   Bar line placement
(Copy 2)

Shield the answer below the notes. Listen to the melody and show where the bar lines should appear; then check your response. Stop the tape between frames. Goal: No more than five incorrect frames.

The following rhythms are in 3/4 meter.

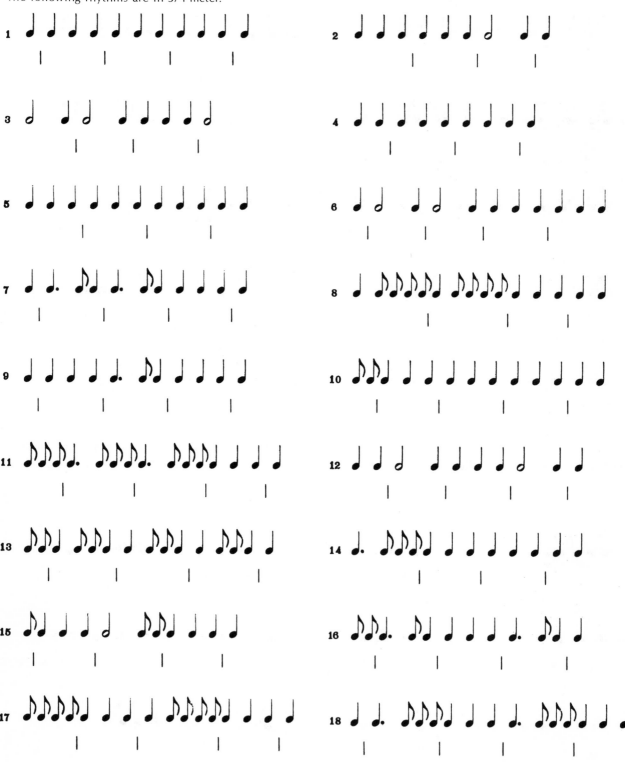

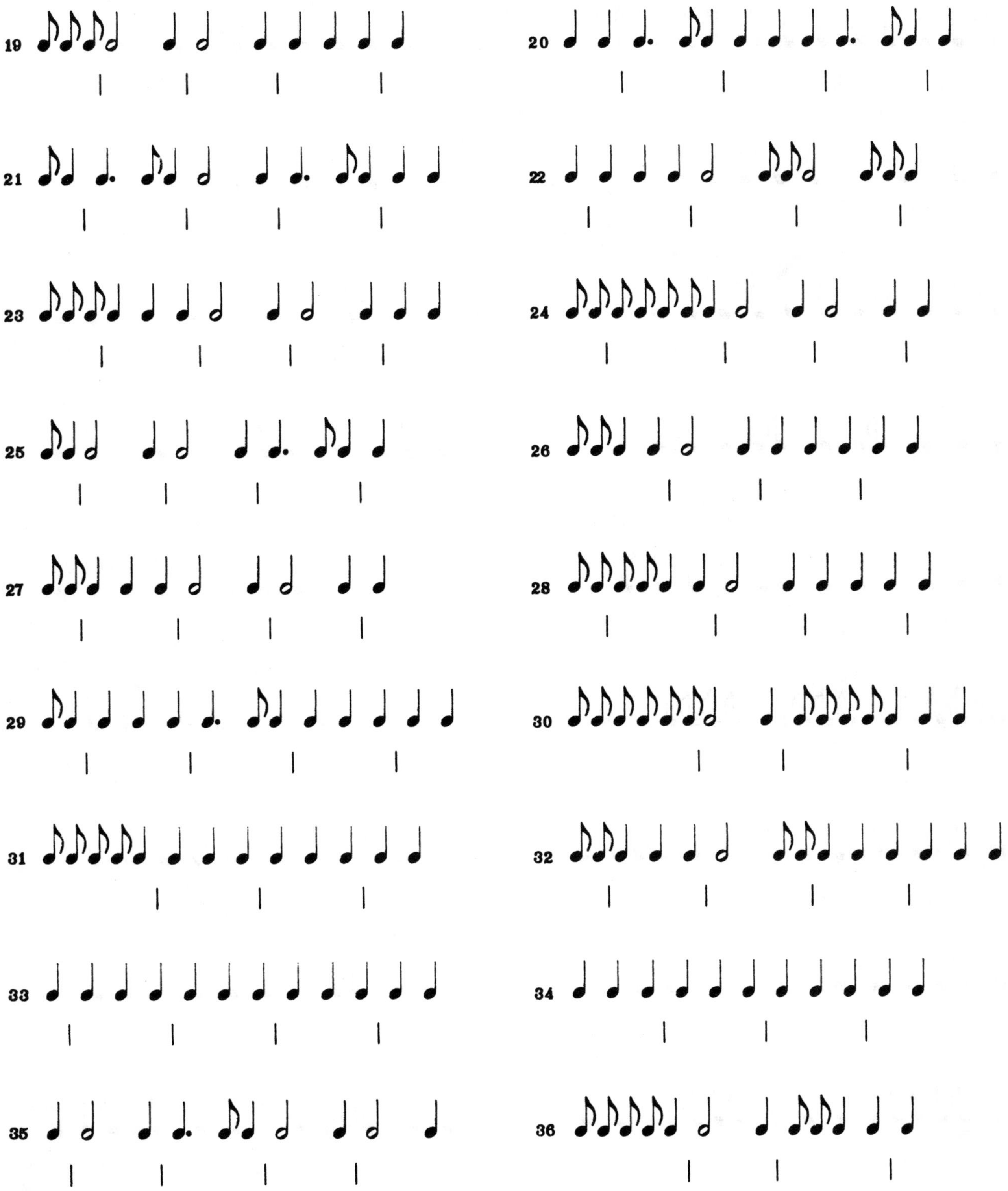
19
20
21
22
23
24
25
26
27
28
29
30
31
32
33
34
35
36

B8-1

(Copy 3)

Bar line placement

Shield the answer below the notes. Listen to the melody and show where the bar lines should appear; then check your response. Stop the tape between frames. Goal: No more than five incorrect frames.

The following rhythms are in 3/4 meter.

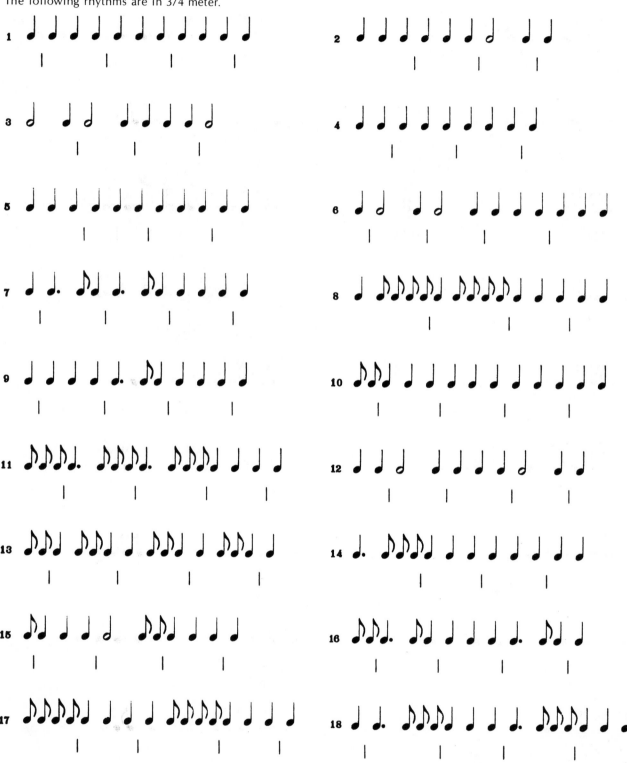

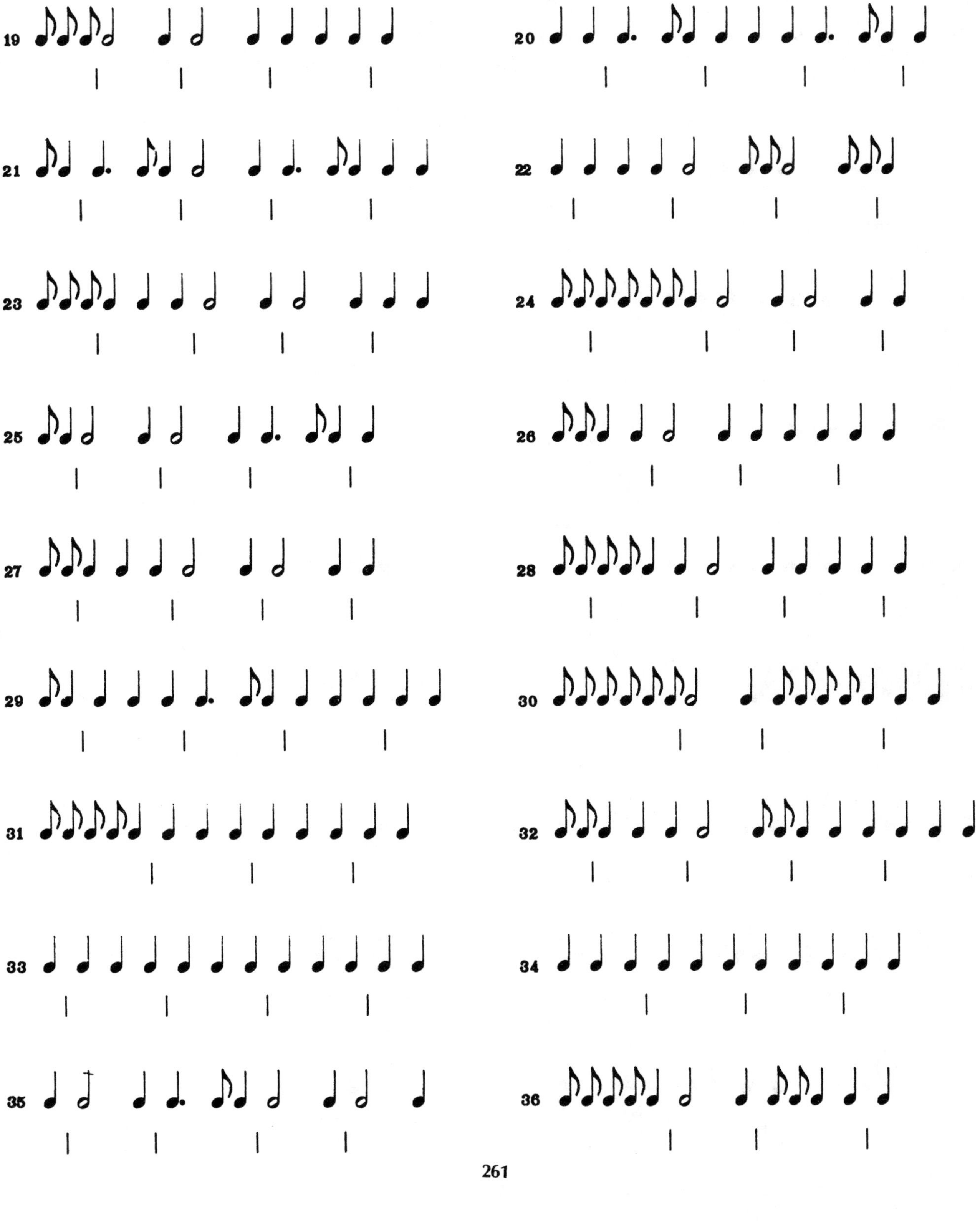
19
20
21
22
23
24
25
26
27
28
29
30
31
32
33
34
35
36

B8-1

(Copy 4)

Bar line placement

Shield the answer below the notes. Listen to the melody and show where the bar lines should appear; then check your response. Stop the tape between frames. Goal: No more than five incorrect frames.

The following rhythms are in 3/4 meter.

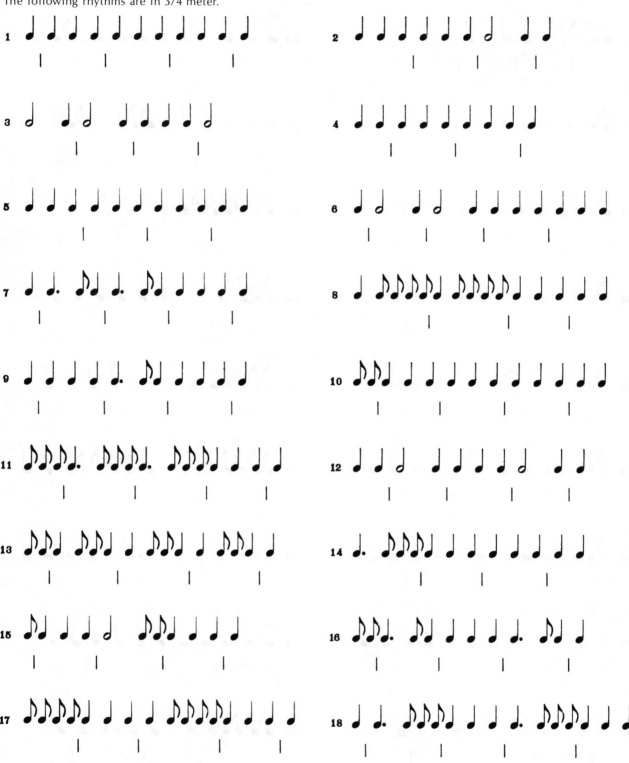

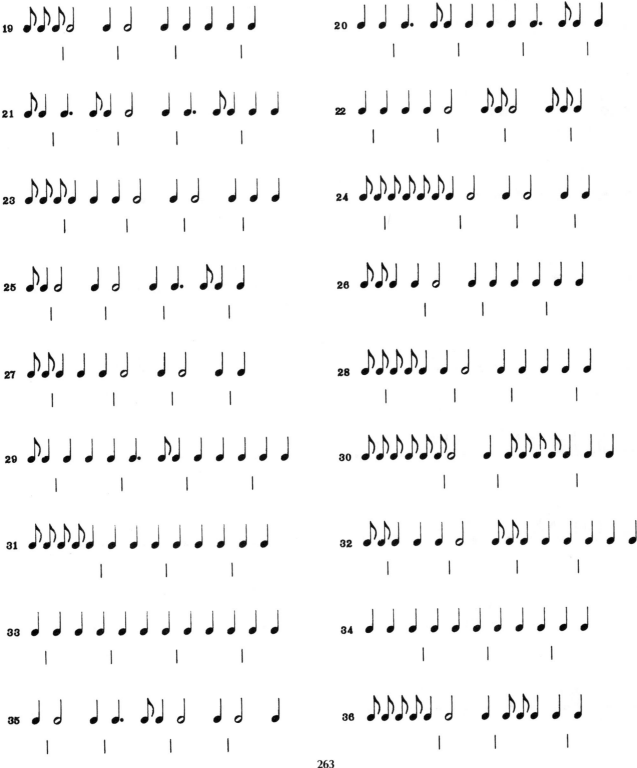

B8-1

(Copy 5)

Bar line placement

Shield the answer below the notes. Listen to the melody and show where the bar lines should appear; then check your response. Stop the tape between frames. Goal: No more than five incorrect frames.

The following rhythms are in 3/4 meter.

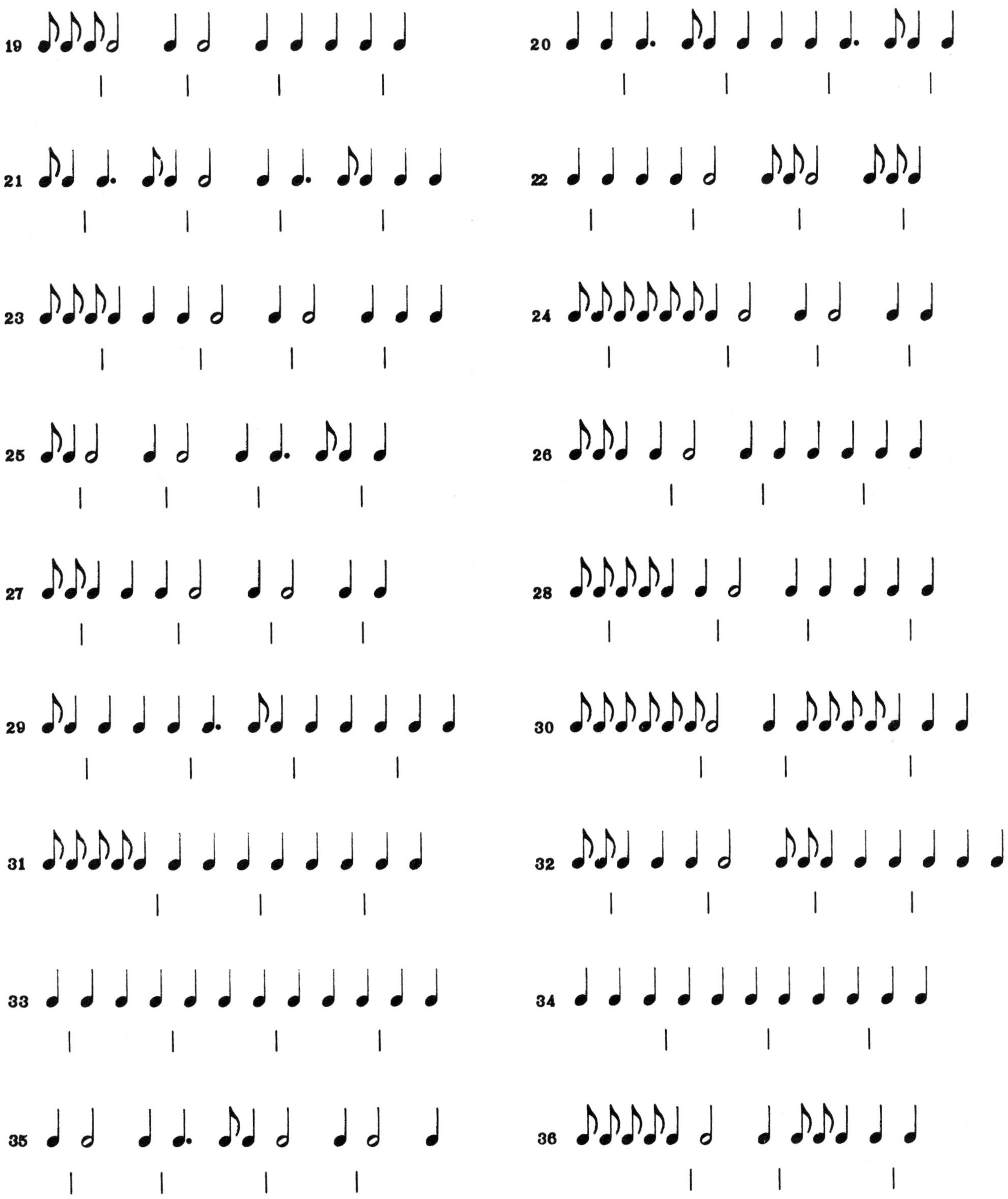
19
20
21
22
23
24
25
26
27
28
29
30
31
32
33
34
35
36

B8-2 Bar line placement
(Copy 1)

Shield the answer below the notes. Listen to the melody and show where the bar lines should appear; then check your response. Stop the tape between frames. Goal: No more than five incorrect frames.

The following rhythms are in 4/4 meter.

The following rhythms are in 2/4 meter.

19 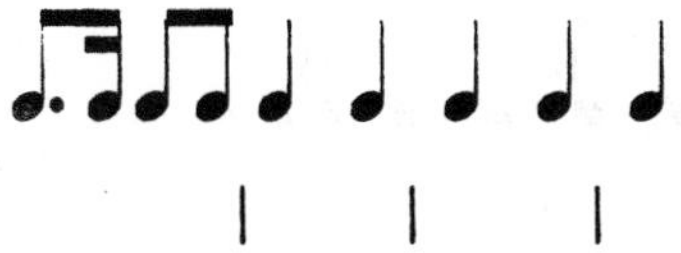

20 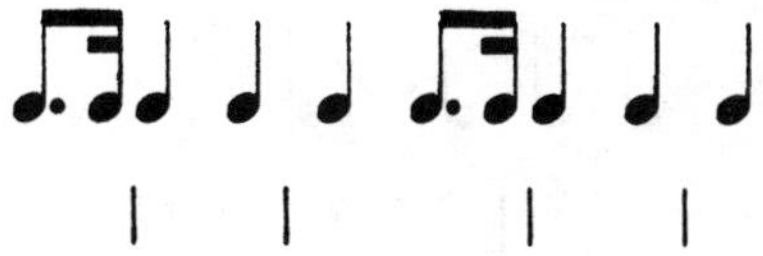

21 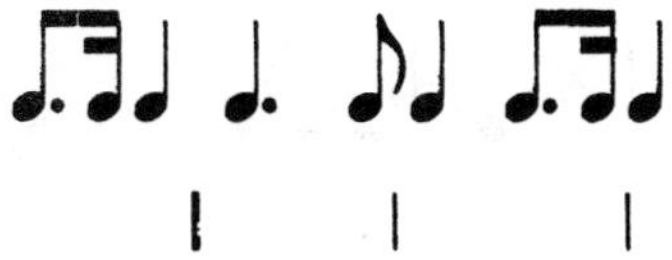

22 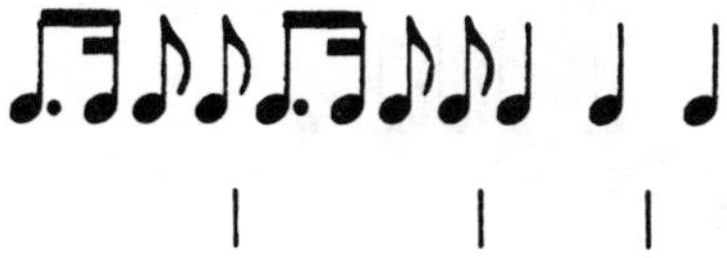

23 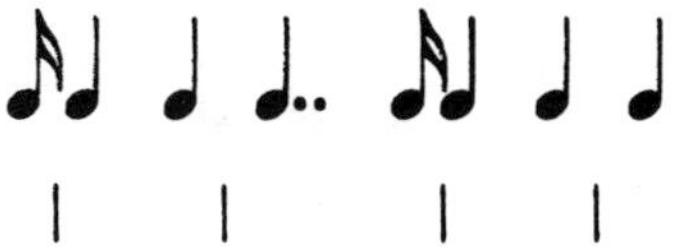

24 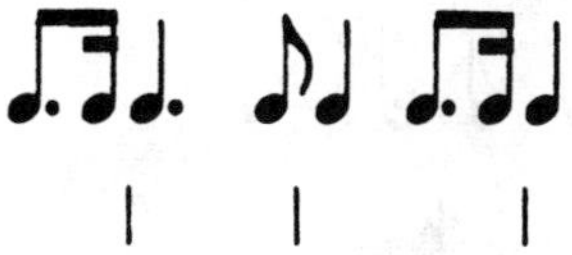

25 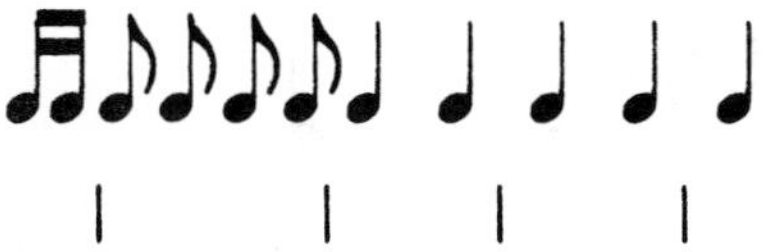

26 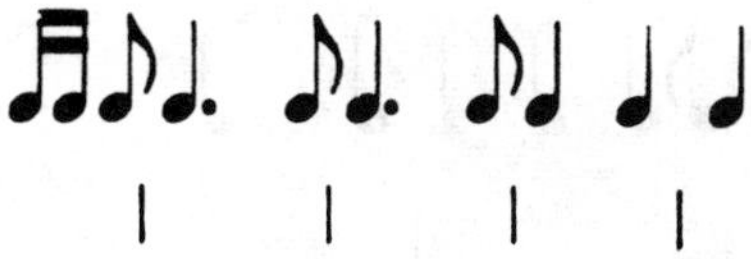

27 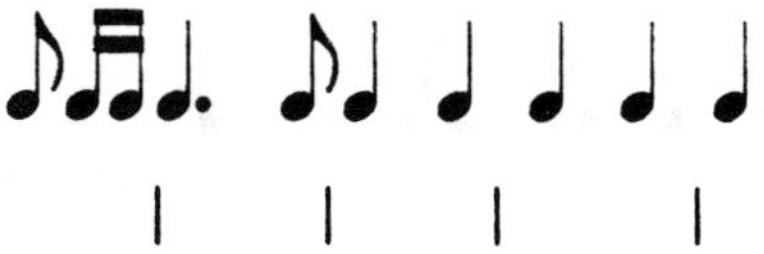

28 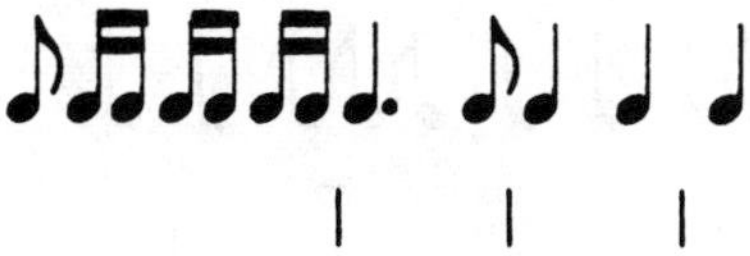

29 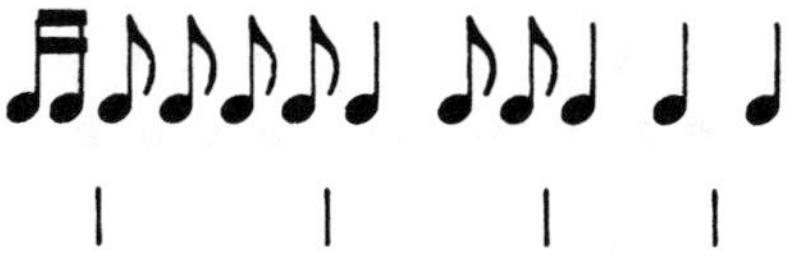

30 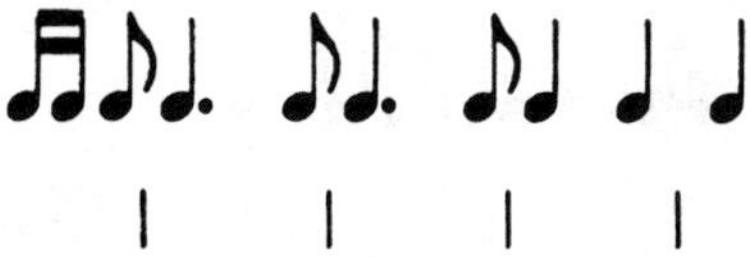

31 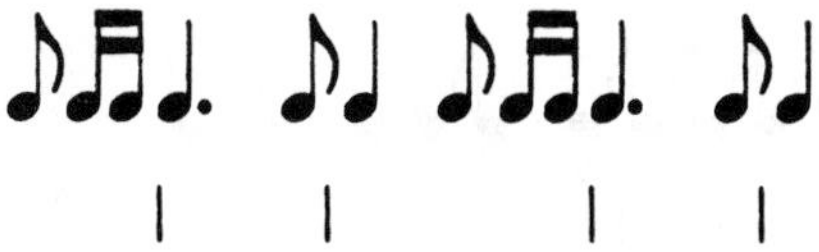

32 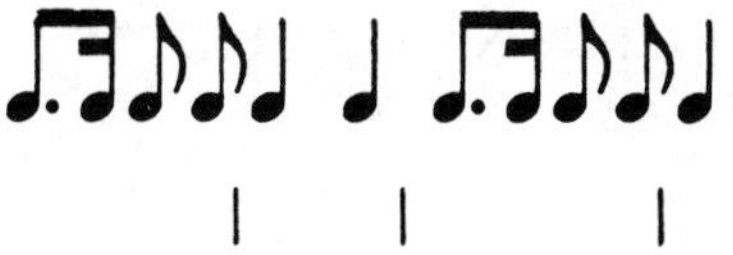

33 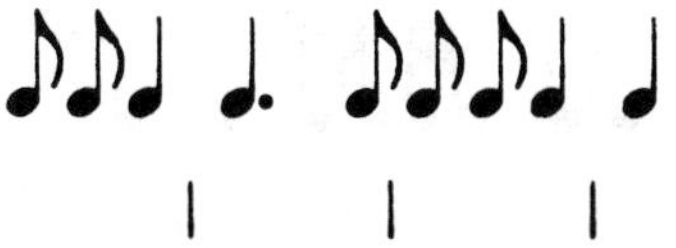

34 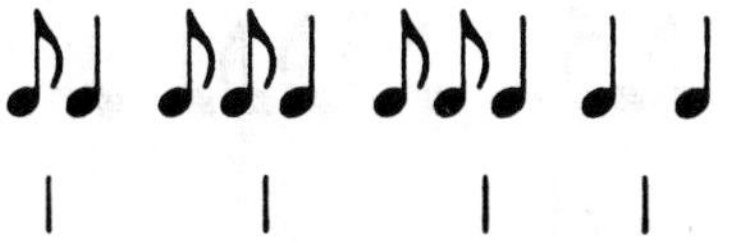

35 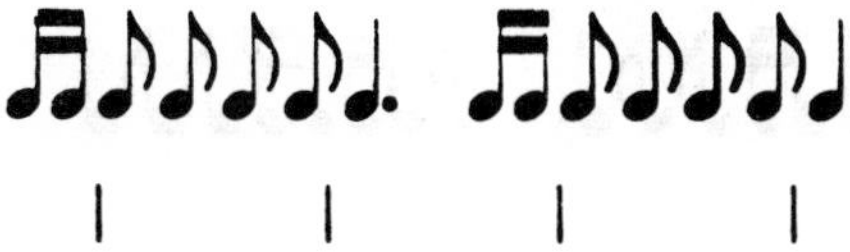

36 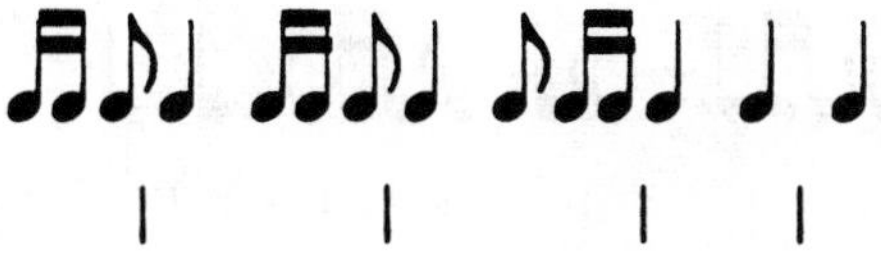

B8-2 Bar line placement

(Copy 2)

Shield the answer below the notes. Listen to the melody and show where the bar lines should appear; then check your response. Stop the tape between frames. Goal: No more than five incorrect frames.

The following rhythms are in 4/4 meter.

The following rhythms are in 2/4 meter.

19 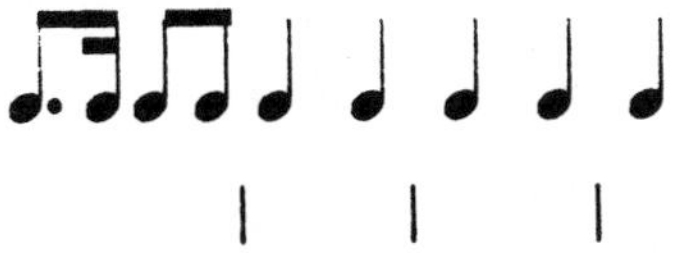

20 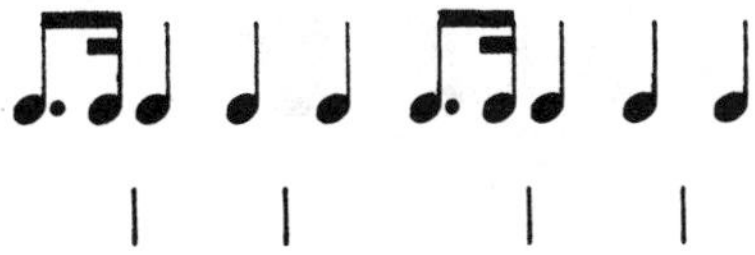

21 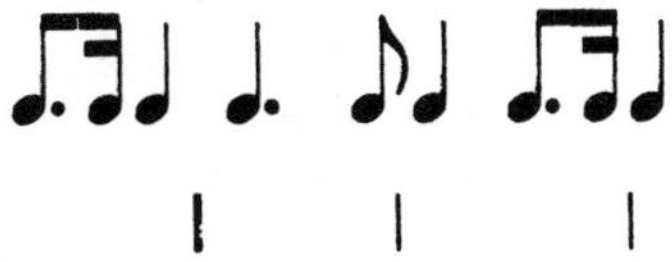

22 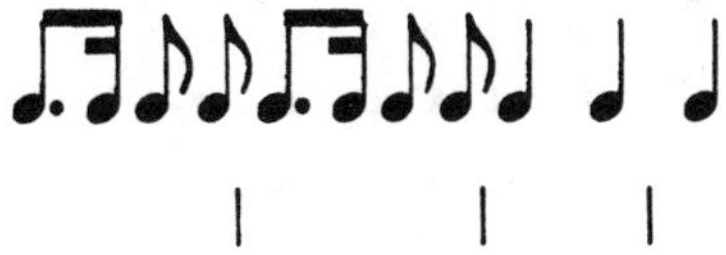

23 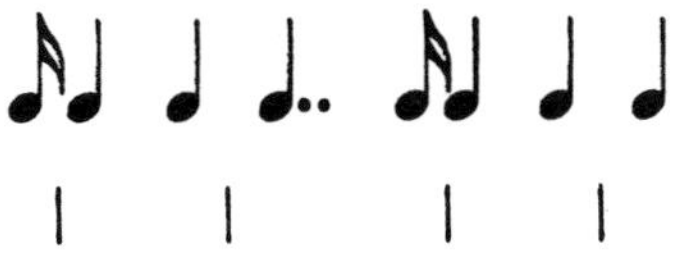

24 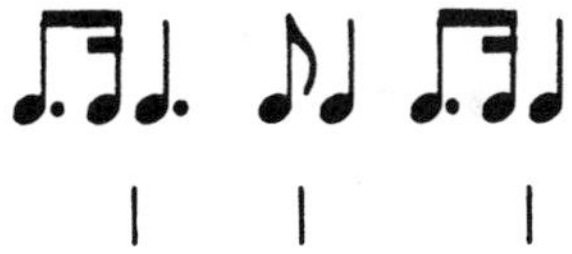

25 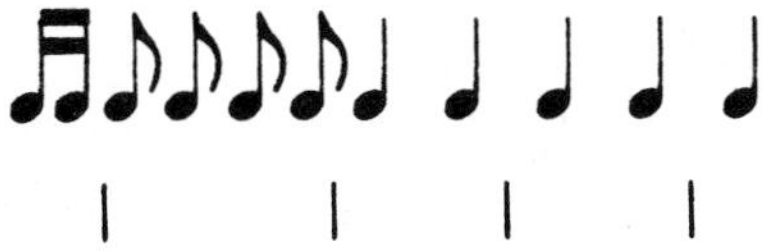

26 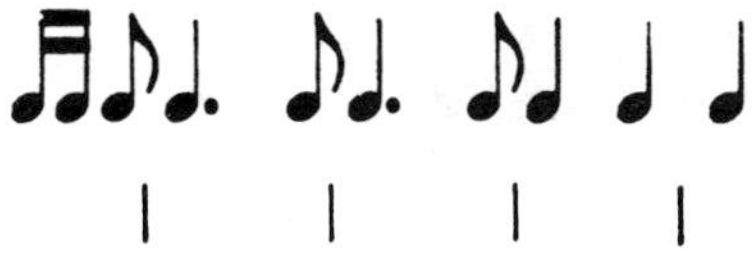

27 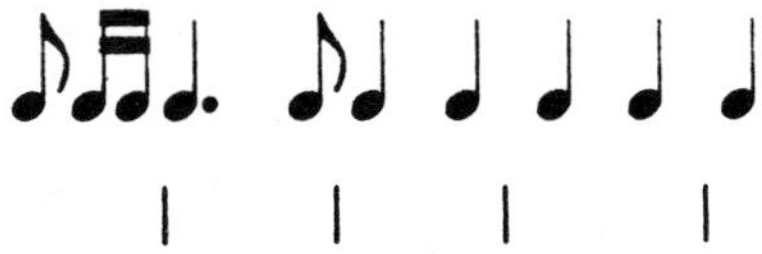

28 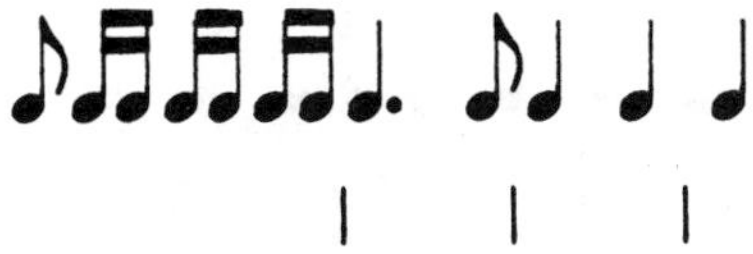

29 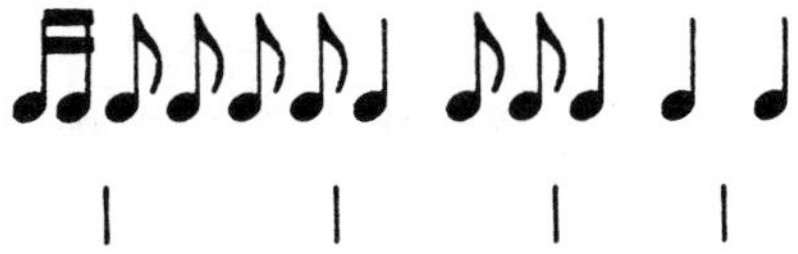

30 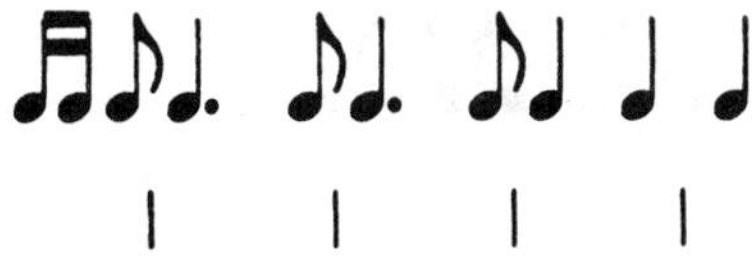

31 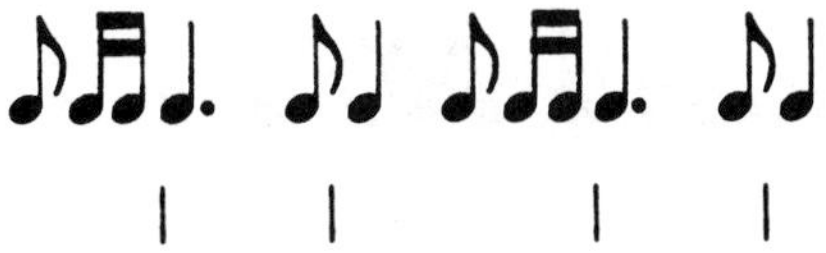

32 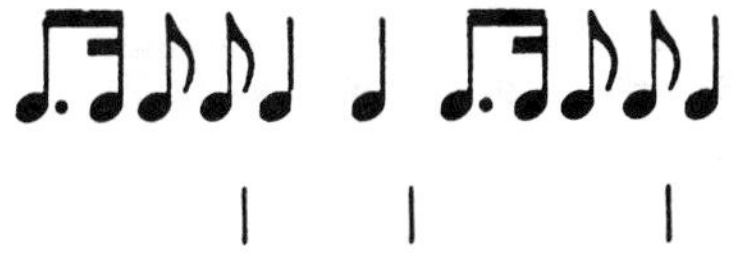

33 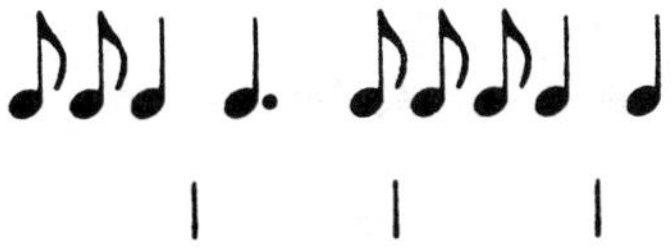

34 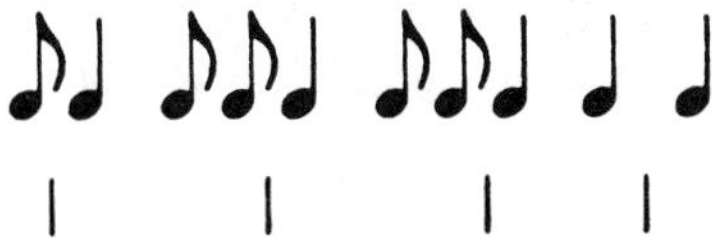

35 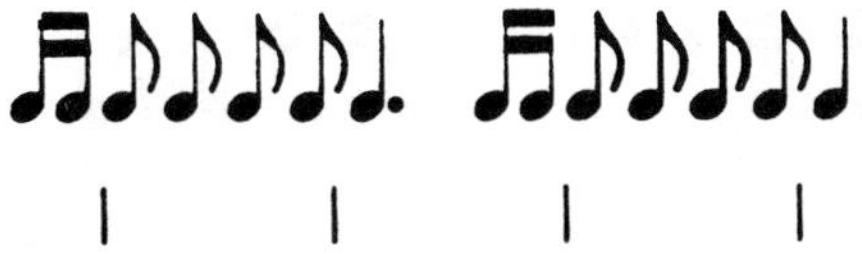

36 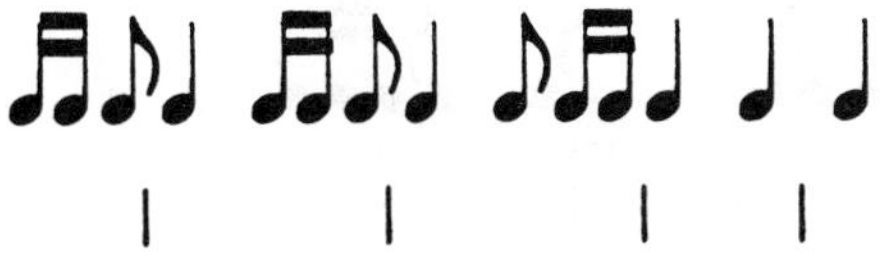

B8-2 Bar line placement

(Copy 3)

Shield the answer below the notes. Listen to the melody and show where the bar lines should appear; then check your response. Stop the tape between frames. Goal: No more than five incorrect frames.

The following rhythms are in 4/4 meter.

The following rhythms are in 2/4 meter.

19 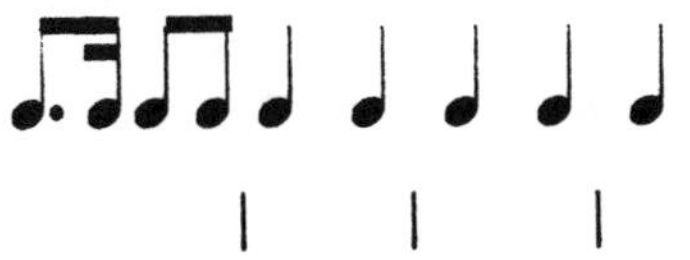

20 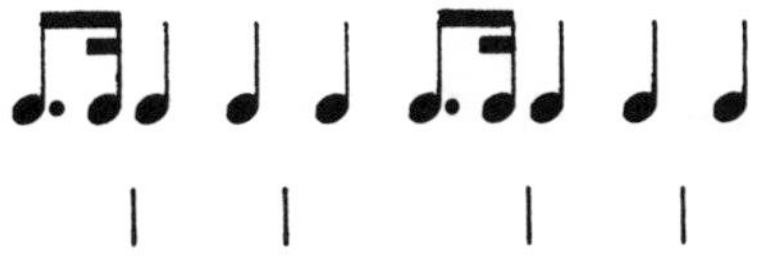

21 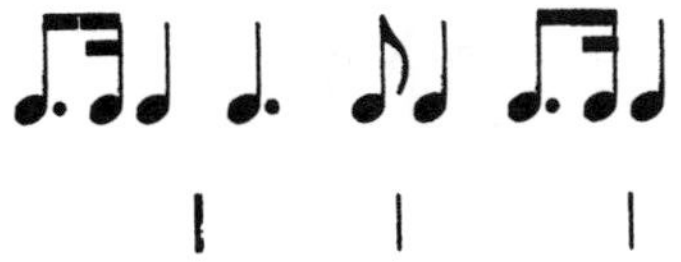

22 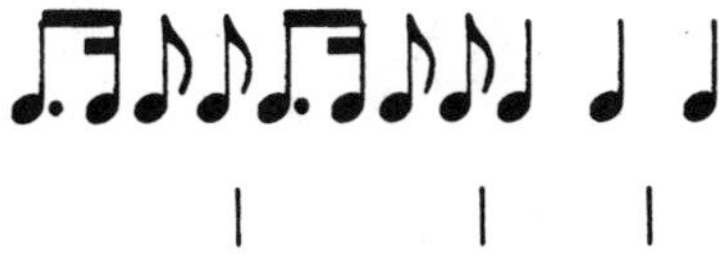

23 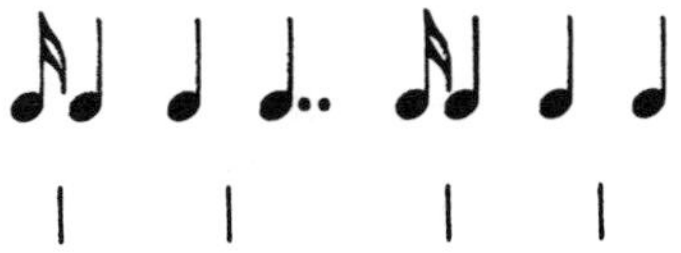

24 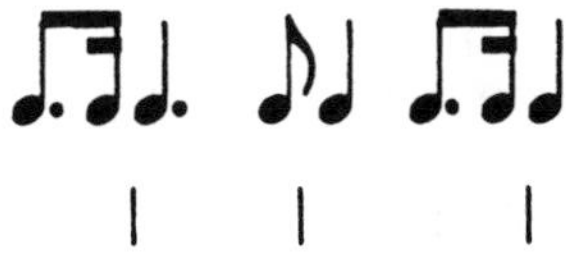

25 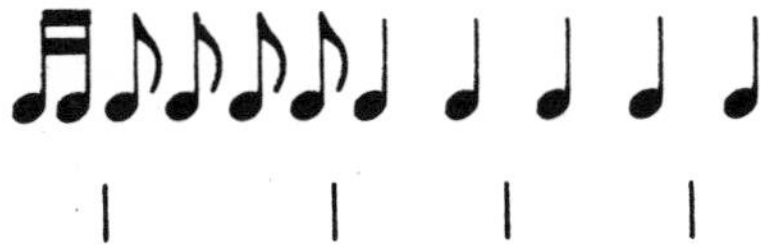

26 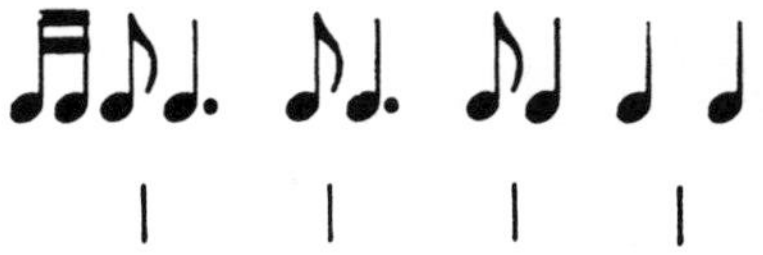

27 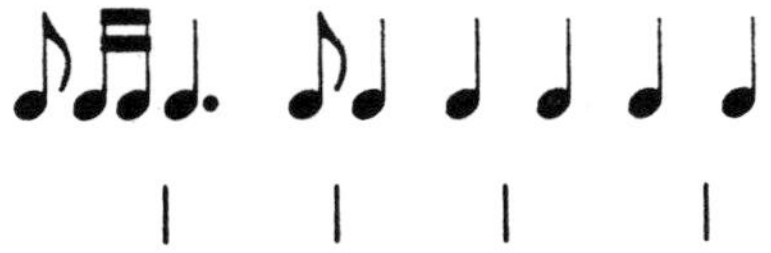

28 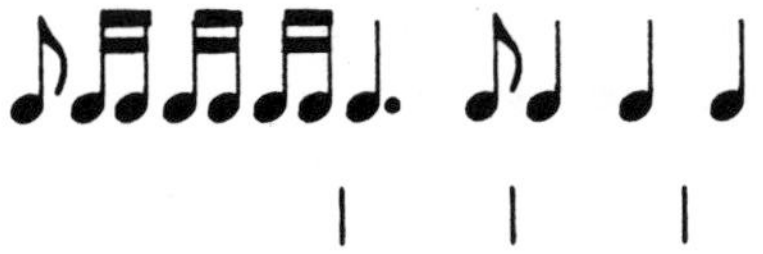

29 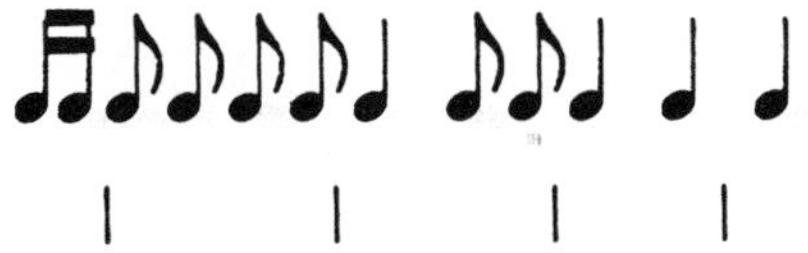

30 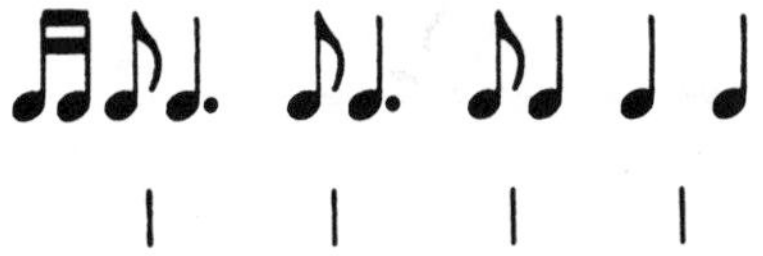

31 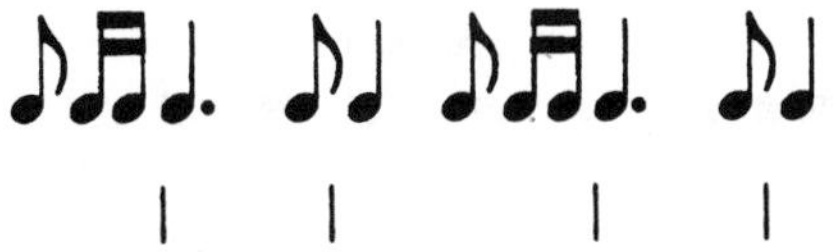

32 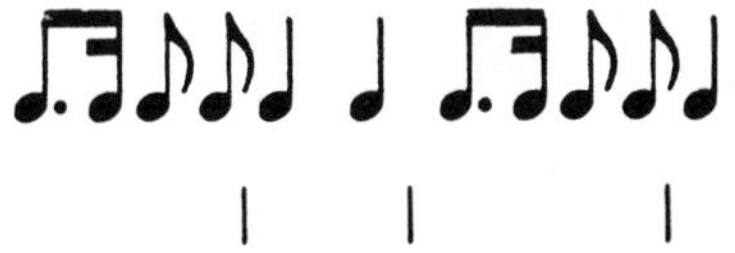

33 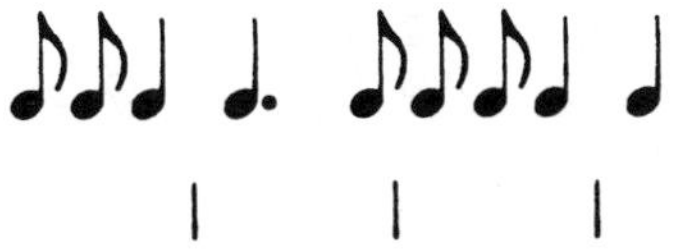

34 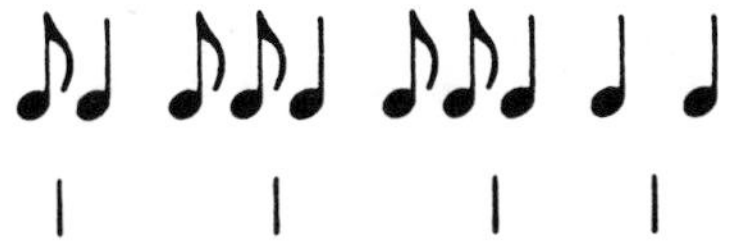

35 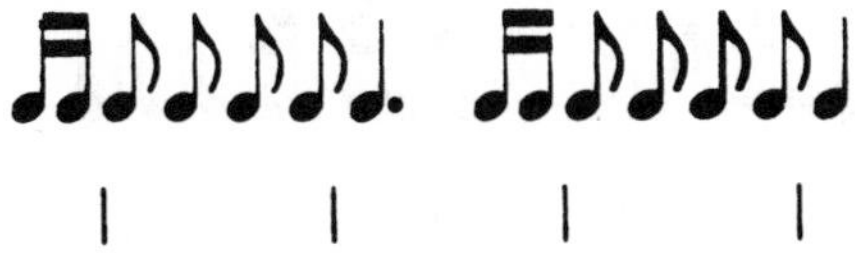

36 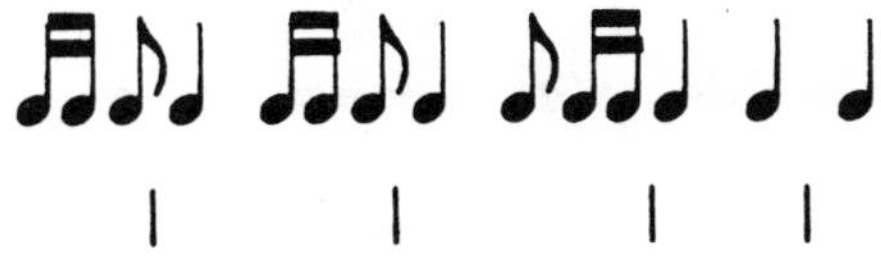

B8-2   Bar line placement
(Copy 4)

Shield the answer below the notes. Listen to the melody and show where the bar lines should appear; then check your response. Stop the tape between frames. Goal: No more than five incorrect frames.

The following rhythms are in 4/4 meter.

1

2

3

4

5

6

7

8

The following rhythms are in 2/4 meter.

9

10

11

12

13

14

15

16

17

18

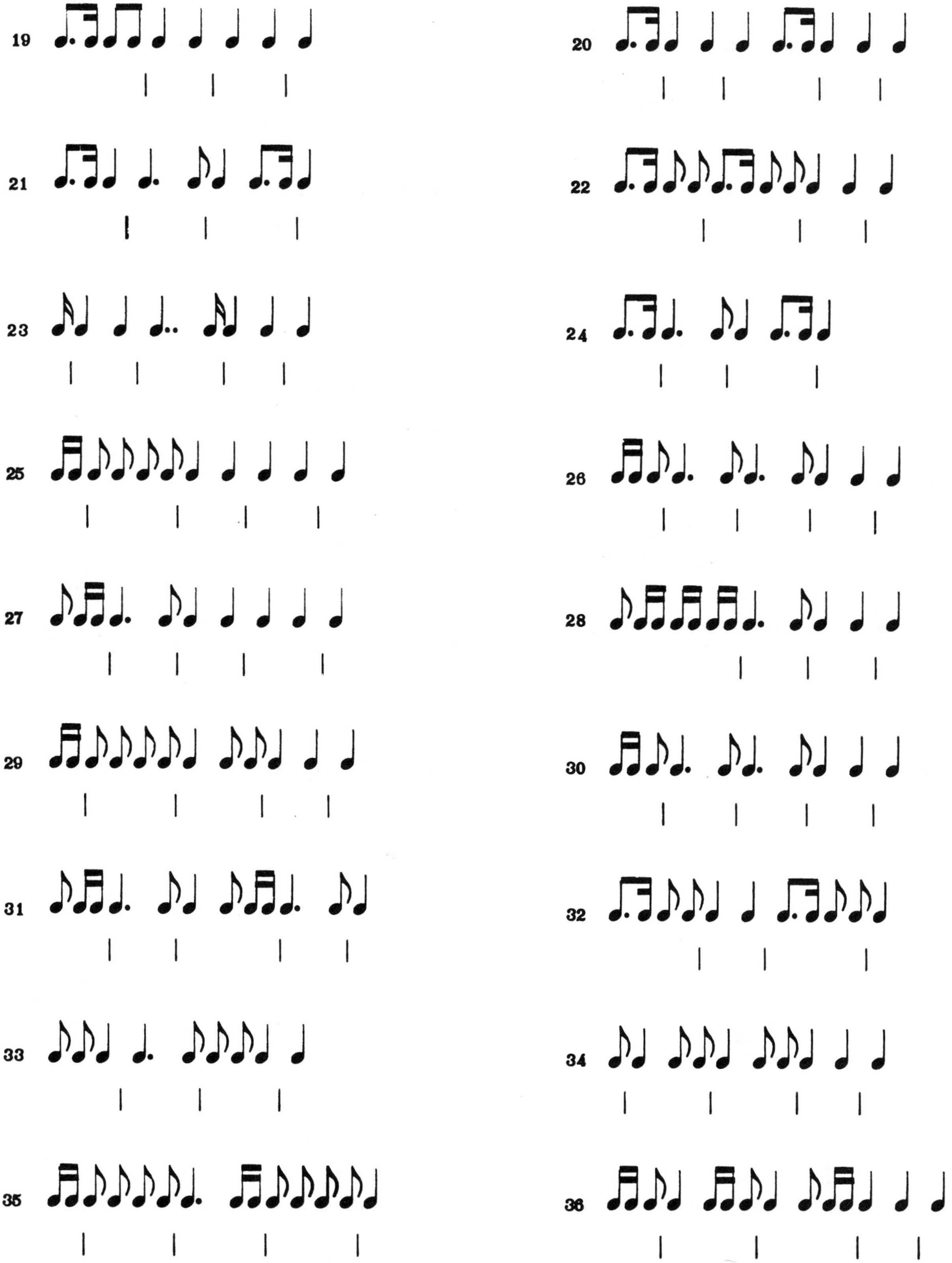
19
20
21
22
23
24
25
26
27
28
29
30
31
32
33
34
35
36

B8-2   Bar line placement
(Copy 5)

*Shield the answer below the notes. Listen to the melody and show where the bar lines should
appear; then check your response. Stop the tape between frames. Goal: No more than five incorrect
frames.*

The following rhythms are in 4/4 meter.

The following rhythms are in 2/4 meter.

274

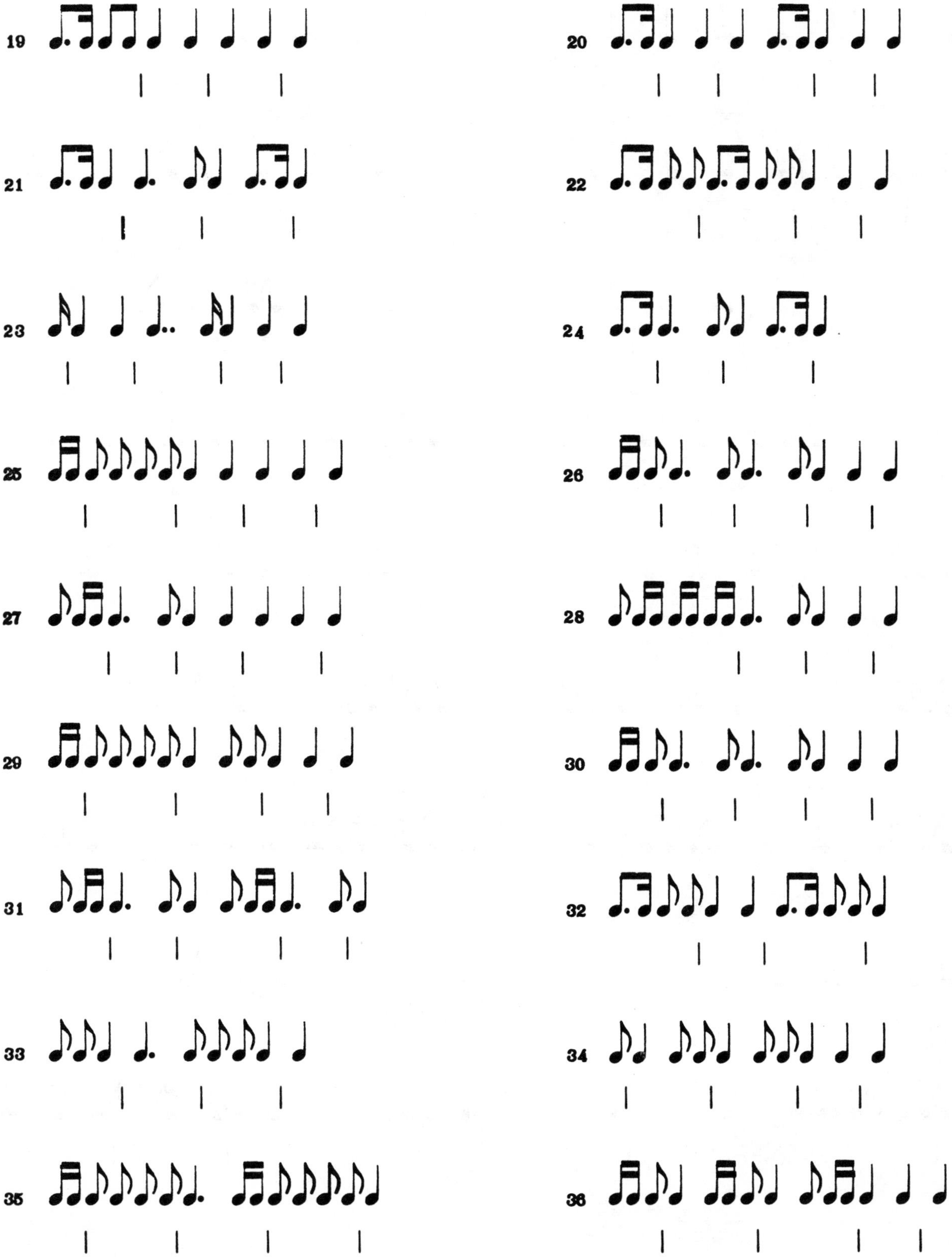
19
20
21
22
23
24
25
26
27
28
29
30
31
32
33
34
35
36

B8-3   Bar line placement
(Copy 1)

Shield the answer below the notes. Listen to the melody and show where the bar lines should appear; then check your response. Stop the tape between frames. Goal: No more than five incorrect frames.

The following rhythms are in 6/8 meter.

The following rhythms are in 2/4 or 6/8 meter.

19 ♪♪♪♪ ♪♪. ♩

20 ♪♪♪♪♪. ♪♪

21 ♪♩ ♪♪♩ ♪♪♩

22 ♪♩ ♪♪♪♪♩ ♪♪♪♪♩

23 ♪♩ ♪♪♩ ♪♪♩

24 ♪♪♩. ♪♪♪♩

25 ♪♩ ♪♩. ♩ ♪♩. ♪♪♪♩

26 ♪♪♩ ♪♪♩. ♪♩

27 ♪♪♩. ♪♩ ♪♪♩. ♪♩

28 ♪♪♩. ♪♩. ♪♩ ♩ ♩

29 ♪♪♪♩. ♪♪♪♩. ♪♪♪♩. ♩. ♩.

30 ♪♪♪♩ ♪♪♪♪♪♪♩. ♪♩

31 ♪♪♩ ♪♪♪♪♩ ♪♪♩ ♩ ♩

32 ♪♪♩. ♪♪♪♩. ♪♪♪♩

33 ♩ ♪♩. ♩ ♪♩. ♪♪♪♩

34 ♪♪♩. ♪♪♪♪♪♪

35 ♪♪♪♩ ♩ ♩ ♪♪♩ ♩ ♩

36 ♪♪♪♩ ♩ ♩ ♩ ♩ ♪♪♩

B8-3 Bar line placement
(Copy 2)

Shield the answer below the notes. Listen to the melody and show where the bar lines should appear; then check your response. Stop the tape between frames. Goal: No more than five incorrect frames.

The following rhythms are in 6/8 meter.

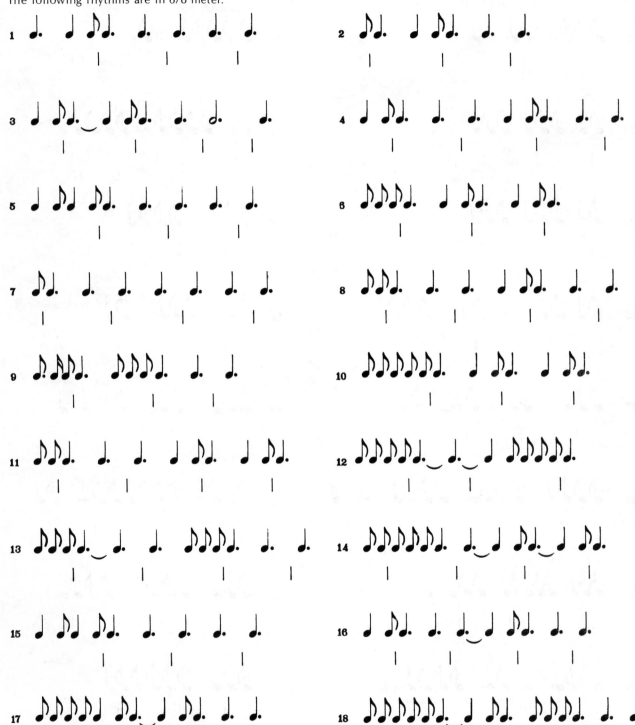

The following rhythms are in 2/4 or 6/8 meter.

19 ♪♪♪♩ ♪♩. ♩

20 ♪♪♪♪♩. ♪♪

21 ♪♩ ♪♪♩ ♪♪♩

22 ♪♩ ♪♪♪♩ ♪♪♪♩

23 ♪♩ ♪♪♩ ♪♪♩

24 ♪♪♩. ♪♪♪♩

25 ♪♩ ♪♩. ♩ ♪♩. ♪♪♪♩

26 ♪♪♩ ♪♪♩. ♪♩

27 ♪♪♩. ♪♩ ♪♪♩. ♪♩

28 ♪♪♩. ♪♩. ♪♩ ♩ ♩

29 ♪♪♪♩. ♪♪♪♩. ♪♪♪♩. ♩. ♩.

30 ♪♪♪♩ ♪♪♪♪♪♩. ♪♩

31 ♪♪♩ ♪♪♪♪♩ ♪♪♩ ♩ ♩

32 ♪♪♩. ♪♪♪♩. ♪♪♪♩

33 ♩ ♪♩. ♩ ♪♩. ♪♪♪♩

34 ♪♪♩. ♪♪♪♪♪♩

35 ♪♪♪♩ ♩ ♩ ♪♪♩ ♩ ♩

36 ♪♪♪♩ ♩ ♩ ♩ ♪♪♩

279

B8-3

(Copy 3)

Bar line placement

Shield the answer below the notes. Listen to the melody and show where the bar lines should appear; then check your response. Stop the tape between frames. Goal: No more than five incorrect frames.

The following rhythms are in 6/8 meter.

The following rhythms are in 2/4 or 6/8 meter.

19 ♪♪♪♪ ♪♩. ♩

20 ♪♪♪♪♩. ♪♩

21 ♪♩ ♪♪♩ ♪♪♩

22 ♪♩ ♪♪♪♩ ♪♪♪♩

23 ♪♩ ♪♪♩ ♪♪♩

24 ♪♪♩. ♪♪♪♩

25 ♪♩ ♪♩. ♩ ♪♩. ♪♪♪♩

26 ♪♪♩ ♪♪♩. ♪♩

27 ♪♪♩. ♪♩ ♪♪♩. ♪♩

28 ♪♪♩. ♪♩. ♪♩ ♩ ♩

29 ♪♪♪♩. ♪♪♪♩. ♪♪♪♩. ♩. ♩.

30 ♪♪♪♩ ♪♪♪♪♪♩. ♪♩

31 ♪♪♩ ♪♪♪♪♩ ♪♪♩ ♩ ♩

32 ♪♪♩. ♪♪♪♩. ♪♪♪♩

33 ♩ ♪♩. ♩ ♪♩. ♪♪♪♩

34 ♪♪♩. ♪♪♪♪♪♩

35 ♪♪♪♩ ♩ ♩ ♪♪♩ ♩ ♩

36 ♪♪♪♩ ♩ ♩ ♩ ♩ ♪♪♩

281

B8-3 Bar line placement
(Copy 4)

Shield the answer below the notes. Listen to the melody and show where the bar lines should appear; then check your response. Stop the tape between frames. Goal: No more than five incorrect frames.

The following rhythms are in 6/8 meter.

The following rhythms are in 2/4 or 6/8 meter.

19 ♪♪♪♩ ♪♩. ♩

20 ♪♪♪♪♩. ♪♩

21 ♪♩ ♪♪♩ ♪♪♩

22 ♪♩ ♪♪♪♩ ♪♪♪♩

23 ♪♩ ♪♪♩ ♪♪♩

24 ♪♪♩. ♪♪♪♩

25 ♪♩ ♪♩. ♩ ♪♩. ♪♪♪♩

26 ♪♪♩ ♪♪♩. ♪♩

27 ♪♪♩. ♪♩ ♪♪♩. ♪♩

28 ♪♪♩. ♪♩. ♪♩ ♩ ♩

29 ♪♪♪♩. ♪♪♪♩. ♪♪♪♩. ♩. ♩.

30 ♪♪♪♩ ♪♪♪♪♪♩. ♪♩

31 ♪♪♩ ♪♪♪♪♩ ♪♪♩ ♩ ♩

32 ♪♪♩. ♪♪♪♩. ♪♪♪♩

33 ♩ ♪♩. ♩ ♪♩. ♪♪♪♩

34 ♪♪♩. ♪♪♪♪♪♩

35 ♪♪♪♩ ♩ ♩ ♪♪♩ ♩ ♩

36 ♪♪♪♩ ♩ ♩ ♩ ♩ ♪♪♩

283

B8-3 Bar line placement
(Copy 5)

Shield the answer below the notes. Listen to the melody and show where the bar lines should appear; then check your response. Stop the tape between frames. Goal: No more than five incorrect frames.

The following rhythms are in 6/8 meter.

The following rhythms are in 2/4 or 6/8 meter.

19 ♪♪♪♩ ♪♩. ♩

20 ♪♪♪♪♩. ♪♩

21 ♪♩ ♪♪♩ ♪♪♩

22 ♪♩ ♪♪♪♪♩ ♪♪♪♪♩

23 ♪♩ ♪♪♩ ♪♪♩

24 ♪♪♩. ♪♪♪♩

25 ♪♩ ♪♩. ♩ ♪♩. ♪♪♪♩

26 ♪♪♩ ♪♪♩. ♪♩

27 ♪♪♩. ♪♩ ♪♪♩. ♪♩

28 ♪♪♩. ♪♩. ♪♩ ♩ ♩

29 ♪♪♪♩. ♪♪♪♩. ♪♪♪♩. ♩. ♩.

30 ♪♪♪♩ ♪♪♪♪♪♩. ♪♩

31 ♪♪♩ ♪♪♪♪♩ ♪♪♩ ♩ ♩

32 ♪♪♩. ♪♪♪♩. ♪♪♪♩

33 ♩ ♪♩. ♩ ♪♩. ♪♪♪♩

34 ♪♪♩. ♪♪♪♪♪♩

35 ♪♪♪♩ ♩ ♩ ♪♪♩ ♩ ♩

36 ♪♪♪♩ ♩ ♩ ♩ ♪♪♩

285

B8-4 Bar line placement

(Copy 1)

Shield the answer below the notes. Listen to the melody and show where the bar lines should appear; then check your response. Stop the tape between frames. Goal: No more than five incorrect frames.

The following rhythms are in 4/4 or 3/4 meter.

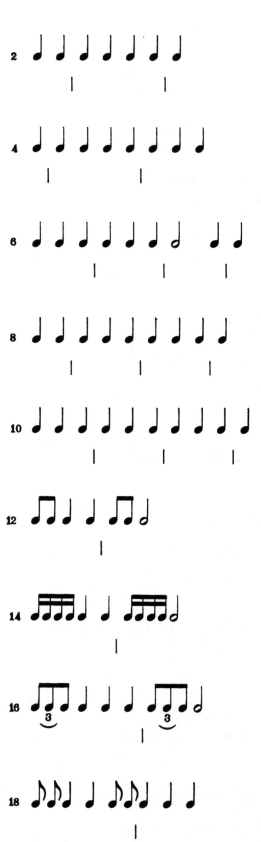

286

The following rhythms are in 2/4 or 3/4 meter.

B8-4 Bar line placement
(Copy 2)

Shield the answer below the notes. Listen to the melody and show where the bar lines should appear; then check your response. Stop the tape between frames. Goal: No more than five incorrect frames.

The following rhythms are in 4/4 or 3/4 meter.

The following rhythms are in 2/4 or 3/4 meter.

19 ♪𝅘𝅥𝅮𝅘𝅥𝅮𝅘𝅥𝅮𝅘𝅥𝅮 ♪♪♪♪

20 𝅘𝅥𝅮𝅘𝅥𝅮♪♪♪ ♪♪♪

21 𝅘𝅥𝅮𝅘𝅥𝅮𝅘𝅥𝅮𝅘𝅥𝅮 ♩ ♩ 𝅘𝅥𝅮𝅘𝅥𝅮 ♩

22 𝅘𝅥𝅮.♪♪ ♩ 𝅘𝅥𝅮.𝅘𝅥𝅮𝅘𝅥𝅮♪

23 ♪𝅘𝅥𝅮𝅘𝅥𝅮♪♪♪𝅘𝅥𝅮♪♪

24 ♪𝅘𝅥𝅮𝅘𝅥𝅮♪♪♪𝅘𝅥𝅮𝅘𝅥𝅮 ♪♪♪

25 ♪♪♩ ♪♪♩ ♪♩

26 𝅘𝅥𝅮𝅘𝅥𝅮♩ ♩ ♩ 𝅘𝅥𝅮𝅘𝅥𝅮♩ ♩

27 ♪𝅘𝅥𝅮𝅘𝅥𝅮♪♪𝅘𝅥𝅮♪♪𝅘𝅥𝅮♪♪𝅘𝅥𝅮♪

28 ♪𝅘𝅥𝅮𝅘𝅥𝅮♪♪𝅘𝅥𝅮♪♪𝅘𝅥𝅮♪

29 ♪𝅘𝅥𝅮𝅘𝅥𝅮♪♪𝅘𝅥𝅮♪♪𝅘𝅥𝅮♪♪𝅘𝅥𝅮♪♪𝅘𝅥𝅮♪

30 ♪𝅘𝅥𝅮𝅘𝅥𝅮♪♪𝅘𝅥𝅮♪♪♪ ♪♪♪

31 𝅘𝅥𝅮𝅘𝅥𝅮𝅘𝅥𝅮𝅘𝅥𝅮𝅘𝅥𝅮♩ ♩ ♩ ♩

32 ♩ 𝅘𝅥𝅮𝅘𝅥𝅮𝅘𝅥𝅮𝅘𝅥𝅮𝅘𝅥𝅮𝅘𝅥𝅮 ♩

33 ♪♪♩ ♩ ♩ ♪♪♩

34 ♪♪♩ ♩ ♪♪♩

35 ♪♪♪♪♪𝅘𝅥𝅮♪♪𝅘𝅥𝅮♪♪♪

36 ♪♪♪♪♪𝅘𝅥𝅮♪♪𝅘𝅥𝅮♪♪♪

B8-4 Bar line placement
(Copy 3)

Shield the answer below the notes. Listen to the melody and show where the bar lines should appear; then check your response. Stop the tape between frames. Goal: No more than five incorrect frames.

The following rhythms are in 4/4 or 3/4 meter.

The following rhythms are in 2/4 or 3/4 meter.

B8-4 Bar line placement
(Copy 4)

Shield the answer below the notes. Listen to the melody and show where the bar lines should appear; then check your response. Stop the tape between frames. Goal: No more than five incorrect frames.

The following rhythms are in 4/4 or 3/4 meter.

The following rhythms are in 2/4 or 3/4 meter.

293

B8-4 Bar line placement
(Copy 5)

Shield the answer below the notes. Listen to the melody, and show where the bar lines should appear; then check your response. Stop the tape between frames. Goal: No more than five incorrect frames.

The following rhythms are in 4/4 or 3/4 meter.

The following rhythms are in 2/4 or 3/4 meter.

Lesson **B8-5**

This is a lesson in *rhythmic dictation of complete phrases*. A worksheet and a tape recording are provided for this lesson. To do each frame, start by shielding the printed answer on the right side of the page. For each melody you hear, you are to write the time signature, bar lines, and note values in the space provided. Each melody appears twice on the tape recording. You may stop the tape while writing your answer. After you have responded, slide the shield down and check your response. Circle each frame in which your response is incorrect. Your goal is to complete each lesson with no more than four incorrect frames. When you have achieved this goal, go on to the next lesson. If you have more than four incorrect frames, repeat the lesson until you reach the goal or until you have done the lesson five times at which point you should go on to the next lesson regardless of the number of errors.

Rhythmic dictation of complete phrases

Shield the answer. Listen to the melody and write the rhythm, time signature, and bar lines; then check your response. Stop the tape between frames. Goal: No more than four incorrect frames. After you have done this lesson, take Test B8.

The following rhythms are in 3/4 or 4/4 meter.

1

2

3

4

5

6

7

8

9

The following rhythms are in 6/8 or 2/4 meter.

10

11

12

13

14

15

16

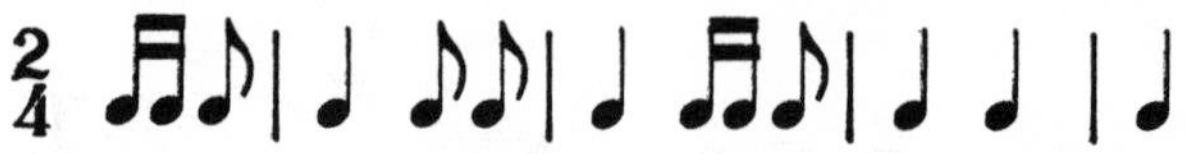

17

18

The following rhythms are in 2/4 or 3/4 meter.

19

20

21

22

23

24

298

Rhythmic dictation of complete phrases

Shield the answer. Listen to the melody and write the rhythm, time signature, and bar lines; then check your response. Stop the tape between frames. Goal: No more than four incorrect frames. After you have done this lesson, take Test B8.

The following rhythms are in 3/4 or 4/4 meter.

1

2

3

4

5

6

7

8

9

The following rhythms are in 6/8 or 2/4 meter.

10

11

12

13

14

15

16

17

18

The following rhythms are in 2/4 or 3/4 meter.

19

20

21

22

23

24

B8-5
(Copy 3)

Rhythmic dictation of complete phrases

Shield the answer. Listen to the melody and write the rhythm, time signature, and bar lines; then check your response. Stop the tape between frames. Goal: No more than four incorrect frames. After you have done this lesson, take Test B8.

The following rhythms are in 3/4 or 4/4 meter.

1

2

3

4

5

6

7

8

9

The following rhythms are in 6/8 or 2/4 meter.

10

11

12

13 $\frac{6}{8}$ ♪| ♩ ♪♩ ♪| ♩. ♩. | ♩. ♩. | ♩.

14 $\frac{2}{4}$ ♪♫| ♩ ♩ | ♩ ♪♪| ♩ ♩ | ♩

15 $\frac{2}{4}$ ♩ ♫♫| ♩. ♪| ♩ ♫♫| ♩

16 $\frac{2}{4}$ ♫♪| ♩ ♪♪| ♩ ♫♪| ♩ ♩ | ♩

17 $\frac{6}{8}$ ♪| ♩ ♪♪♪♪| ♩. ♩. | ♩. ♩ ♪| ♩.

18 $\frac{2}{4}$ ♫| ♩ ♪♪| ♩ ♪♪| ♪♪♪ | ♩

The following rhythms are in 2/4 or 3/4 meter.

19 $\frac{2}{4}$ ♩ | ♩ ♩ | ♩ ♩ | ♩ ♩ | ♩

20 $\frac{3}{4}$ ♩ ♩ ♩ | ♩ ♩ ♩ | ♩ ♩ ♩ | ♩

21 $\frac{3}{4}$ ♩ ♩ | ♩ ♩ ♩ | ♩ ♩ ♩ | ♩ ♩ ♩ | ♩

22 $\frac{2}{4}$ ♩ ♩ | ♩ ♩ | ♩ ♩ | ♩ ♩ | ♩

23 $\frac{3}{4}$ ♫| ♫ ♫♩ | ♩ ♫ ♫| ♩

24 $\frac{2}{4}$ ♪| ♫ ♫| ♫ ♫| ♩

B8-5

(Copy 4)

Rhythmic dictation of complete phrases

Shield the answer. Listen to the melody and write the rhythm, time signature, and bar lines; then check your response. Stop the tape between frames. Goal: No more than four incorrect frames. After you have done this lesson, take Test B8.

The following rhythms are in 3/4 or 4/4 meter.

1

2

3

4

5

6

7

8

9

The following rhythms are in 6/8 or 2/4 meter.

10

11

12

13

14

15

16

17

18

The following rhythms are in 2/4 or 3/4 meter.

19

20

21

22

23

24

B8-5
(Copy 5)

Rhythmic dictation of complete phrases

Shield the answer. Listen to the melody and write the rhythm, time signature, and bar lines; then check your response. Stop the tape between frames. Goal: No more than four incorrect frames. After you have done this lesson, take Test B8.

The following rhythms are in 3/4 or 4/4 meter.

1

2

3

4

5

6

7

8

9

The following rhythms are in 6/8 or 2/4 meter.

10

11

12

13

$\begin{matrix}6\\8\end{matrix}$ ♪| ♩ ♪♩ ♪| ♩. ♩. | ♩. ♩. | ♩.

14

$\begin{matrix}2\\4\end{matrix}$ ♪♫| ♩ ♩ | ♩ ♪♪| ♩ ♩ | ♩

15

$\begin{matrix}2\\4\end{matrix}$ ♩ ♫♫| ♩. ♪| ♩ ♫♫| ♩

16

$\begin{matrix}2\\4\end{matrix}$ ♫♪| ♩ ♪♪| ♩ ♫♪| ♩ ♩ | ♩

17

$\begin{matrix}6\\8\end{matrix}$ ♪| ♩ ♪♪♪♪| ♩. ♩. | ♩. ♩ ♪| ♩.

18

$\begin{matrix}2\\4\end{matrix}$ ♫| ♩ ♪♪| ♩ ♪♪| ♪♪♪ | ♩

The following rhythms are in 2/4 or 3/4 meter.

19

$\begin{matrix}2\\4\end{matrix}$ ♩ | ♩ ♩ | ♩ ♩ | ♩ ♩ | ♩

20

$\begin{matrix}3\\4\end{matrix}$ ♩ ♩ ♩ | ♩ ♩ ♩ | ♩ ♩ ♩ | ♩

21

$\begin{matrix}3\\4\end{matrix}$ ♩ ♩ | ♩ ♩ ♩ | ♩ ♩ ♩ | ♩ ♩ ♩ | ♩

22

$\begin{matrix}2\\4\end{matrix}$ ♩ ♩ | ♩ ♩ | ♩ ♩ | ♩ ♩ | ♩

23

$\begin{matrix}3\\4\end{matrix}$ ♫| ♫ ♫♩ | ♩ ♫ ♫♩| ♩

24

$\begin{matrix}2\\4\end{matrix}$ ♪| ♫ ♫| ♫ ♫| ♩

306

Dictation—Complete Phrases

In this series there are five lessons in *melodic dictation of complete phrases.* The purpose of this series is to develop your ability to notate the pitches and rhythm of long melodies that you hear. A worksheet and a tape recording are provided for each lesson. Each frame on the worksheet takes one complete line. The clef and starting note for each melody appear at the beginning of the line. Write these on your own manuscript paper before listening to the melody. Then, while shielding the answer that follows, listen to the melody and write the key signature, time signature, bar lines, and notes. Two time signatures are printed after the initial material. Choose the one for your response that is appropriate for the melody. Stop the tape at the conclusion of the melody. Each melody is recorded twice on the tape recording. You may rewind the tape if you desire additional hearings. On the test for this series, each melody will be heard four times so you should attempt to complete each frame in no more than four hearings. When you have completed your response, compare it to the printed answer. Each lesson in this series should be done only once in preparation for the test. The test itself will serve to measure your achievement. If you wish to raise your test score, you should do each of the lessons once more and then take the test again.

When you have done this series, take Test B9.

B9-1   Melodic dictation of complete phrases

Write the initial material on your own manuscript paper. The melody appears twice on the tape. Rewind the tape for additional hearings. Write the key signature, time signature, bar lines, and notes; then check your response. Do this lesson once in preparation for the test.

B9-2   Melodic dictation of complete phrases

Write the initial material on your own manuscript paper. The melody appears twice on the tape.
Rewind the tape for additional hearings. Write the key signature, time signature, bar lines, and
notes; then check your response. Do this lesson once in preparation for the test.

B9-3 Melodic dictation of complete phrases

Write the initial material on your own manuscript paper. The melody appears twice on the tape. Rewind the tape for additional hearings. Write the key signature, time signature, bar lines, and notes; then check your response. Do this lesson once in preparation for the test.

310

B9-4   Melodic dictation of complete phrases

Write the initial material on your own manuscript paper. The melody appears twice on the tape.
Rewind the tape for additional hearings. Write the key signature, time signature, bar lines, and
notes; then check your response. Do this lesson once in preparation for the test.

B9-5 Melodic dictation of complete phrases

Write the initial material on your own manuscript paper. The melody appears twice on the tape. Rewind the tape for additional hearings. Write the key signature, time signature, bar lines, and notes; then check your response. Do this lesson once in preparation for the test. After you have done this lesson, take Test B9.

Sightsinging—Skips and Accidentals

In this series, there are three *sightsinging lessons*. The procedure for the lessons in this series is the same as for Series B2: a printed worksheet and a tape recording are provided for each lesson. The frames on the worksheet are separated by double bar lines. You will hear the starting note only for the first frame. For all other frames you must find the first note with reference to the preceding frame. To do each frame, sing the printed melody in time with the metronome. You will then hear the melody correctly performed. Whenever you have not sung a melody correctly, make a tally mark on a piece of paper. Your goal is to have no more than eight incorrect frames in an entire lesson. When you have done so, go on to the next lesson. If you have more than eight incorrect frames, repeat the lesson until you reach the goal or until you have done the lesson five times, at which point you should go on to the next lesson regardless of the number of errors.

When you have done this series, take Test B10.

B10-1 Sightsinging

Sing each frame in time with the metronome and compare your response with the melody you then hear. The starting tone is given for the first frame only. Tally errors on a separate sheet of paper. Goal: No more than eight incorrect frames.

B10-2 Sightsinging

Sing each frame in time with the metronome and compare your response with the melody you then hear. The starting tone is given for the first frame only. Tally errors on a separate sheet of paper. Goal: No more than eight incorrect frames. After you have done this lesson, take Test B10.

316

317

B10-3 Sightsinging

Sing each frame in time with the metronome and compare your response with the melody you then hear. The starting tone is given for the first frame only. Tally errors on a separate sheet of paper. Goal: No more than eight incorrect frames. After you have done this lesson, take Test B10.

318

319

Dictation—Skips and Accidentals   SERIES B11

In this series, there are three *melodic dictation lessons*. The procedure for these lessons is the same as for Series B3: a printed worksheet and a tape recording are provided for each lesson. To do each frame, start by shielding the printed answer. When you have heard the melody, stop the tape and write the notes for the melody. Then slide the shield to the right and compare your response with the printed answer. Circle each frame in which your response is incorrect. Your goal is to complete each lesson with no more than eight incorrect frames. When you have reached this goal, go on to the next lesson. If you have more than eight incorrect frames, repeat the lesson until you reach the goal or until you have done the lesson five times, at which point you should go on to the next lesson regardless of the number of errors.

When you have done this series, take Test B11.

B11-1 Melodic dictation

(Copy 1)

Shield the answer. Listen to the melody and notate it; then check your response. Circle incorrect responses. Stop the tape between frames. Goal: No more than eight incorrect frames.

323

B11-1 Melodic dictation

(Copy 2)

Shield the answer. Listen to the melody and notate it; then check your response. Circle incorrect responses. Stop the tape between frames. Goal: No more than eight incorrect frames.

326

327

B11-1 Melodic dictation

(Copy 3)

Shield the answer. Listen to the melody and notate it; then check your response. Circle incorrect responses. Stop the tape between frames. Goal: No more than eight incorrect frames.

329

B11-1 Melodic dictation

(Copy 4)

Shield the answer. Listen to the melody and notate it; then check your response. Circle incorrect responses. Stop the tape between frames. Goal: No more than eight incorrect frames.

331

332

333

B11-1 Melodic dictation

(Copy 5)

Shield the answer. Listen to the melody and notate it; then check your response. Circle incorrect responses. Stop the tape between frames. Goal: No more than eight incorrect frames.

335

B11-2 Melodic dictation

(Copy 1)

Shield the answer. Listen to the melody and notate it; then check your response. Circle incorrect responses. Stop the tape between frames. Goal: No more than eight incorrect frames.

338

339

B11-2 Melodic dictation

(Copy 2)

Shield the answer. Listen to the melody and notate it; then check your response. Circle incorrect responses. Stop the tape between frames. Goal: No more than eight incorrect frames.

341

B11-2 Melodic dictation

(Copy 3)

Shield the answer. Listen to the melody and notate it; then check your response. Circle incorrect responses. Stop the tape between frames. Goal: No more than eight incorrect frames.

344

345

B11-2 Melodic dictation

(Copy 4)

Shield the answer. Listen to the melody and notate it; then check your response. Circle incorrect responses. Stop the tape between frames. Goal: No more than eight incorrect frames.

B11-2 Melodic dictation

(Copy 5)

Shield the answer. Listen to the melody and notate it; then check your response. Circle incorrect responses. Stop the tape between frames. Goal: No more than eight incorrect frames.

350

351

B11-3 Melodic dictation

(Copy 1)

Shield the answer. Listen to the melody and notate it; then check your response. Circle incorrect responses. Stop the tape between frames. Goal: No more than eight incorrect trames. After you have done this lesson, take Test B11.

353

354

B11-3 Melodic dictation

(Copy 2)

Shield the answer. Listen to the melody and notate it; then check your response. Circle incorrect responses. Stop the tape between frames. Goal: No more than eight incorrect frames. After you have done this lesson, take Test B11.

356

357

B11-3 Melodic dictation

(Copy 3)

Shield the answer. Listen to the melody and notate it; then check your response. Circle incorrect responses. Stop the tape between frames. Goal: No more than eight incorrect frames. After you have done this lesson, take Test B11.

358

359

360

B11-3 Melodic dictation

(Copy 4)

Shield the answer. Listen to the melody and notate it; then check your response. Circle incorrect responses. Stop the tape between frames. Goal: No more than eight incorrect frames. After you have done this lesson, take Test B11.

363

B11-3 Melodic dictation

(Copy 5)

Shield the answer. Listen to the melody and notate it; then check your response. Circle incorrect responses. Stop the tape between frames. Goal: No more than eight incorrect frames. After you have done this lesson, take Test B11.

364

365

Sightsinging—Modulations   **SERIES B12**

In this series, there are three *sightsinging lessons*. The procedure for the lessons in this series is the same as for Series B2: a printed worksheet and a tape recording are provided for each lesson. The frames on the worksheet are separated by double bar lines. You will hear the starting note only for the first frame. For all other frames you must find the first note by referring to the preceding frame. To do each frame, sing the printed melody in time with the metronome. You will then hear the melody correctly performed. Whenever you have not sung a melody correctly, make a tally mark on a piece of paper. Your goal is to have no more than eight incorrect frames in an entire lesson. When you have done so, go on to the next lesson. If you have more than eight incorrect frames, repeat the lesson until you reach the goal or until you have done the lesson five times, at which point you should go on to the next lesson regardless of the number of errors.

When you have done this series, take Test B12.

B12-1 Sightsinging

Sing each frame in time with the metronome and compare your response with the melody you then hear. The starting tone is given for the first frame only. Tally errors on a separate sheet of paper. Goal: No more than eight incorrect frames.

369

B12-2 Sightsinging

Sing each frame in time with the metronome and compare your response with the melody you then hear. The starting tone is given for the first frame only. Tally errors on a separate sheet of paper. Goal: No more than eight incorrect frames.

370

371

B12-3 Sightsinging

Sing each frame in time with the metronome and compare your response with the melody you then hear. The starting tone is given for the first frame only. Tally errors on a separate sheet of paper. Goal: No more than eight incorrect frames. After you have done this lesson, take Test B12.

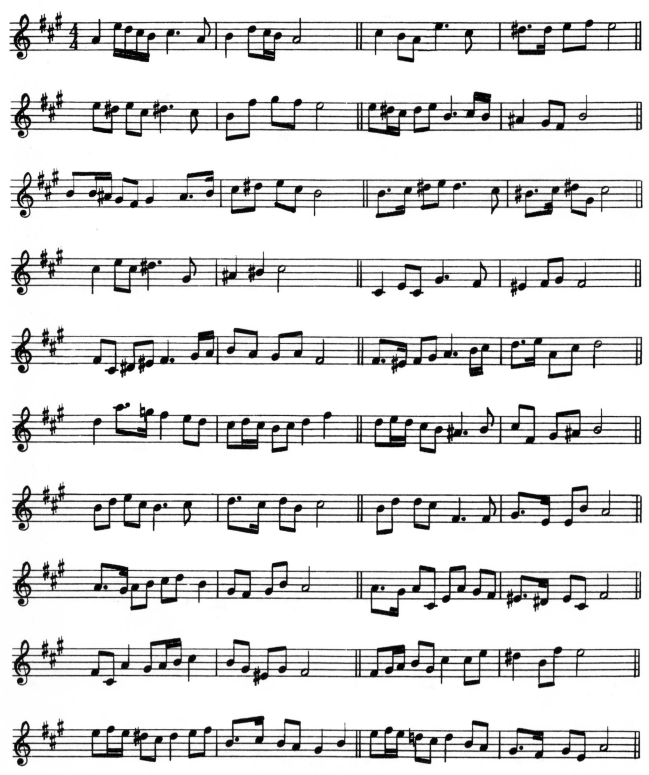

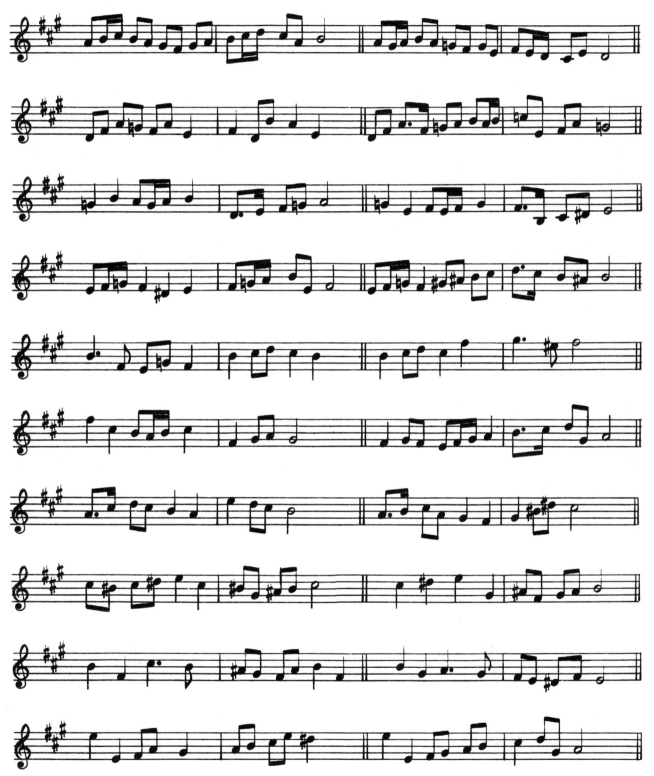

373

Advanced Sightsinging— Melody and Rhythm

In this series, there are nine *sightsinging lessons*. The procedure for these is the same as for Series B2: a printed worksheet and a tape recording are provided for each lesson. The frames on the worksheet are separated by double bar lines. You will hear the starting note only for the first frame. For all other frames you must find the first note with reference to the preceding frame. To do each frame, sing the printed melody in time with the metronome. You will then hear the melody correctly performed. Whenever you have not sung a melody correctly, make a tally mark on a piece of paper. Your goal is to have no more than eight incorrect frames in an entire lesson. When you have done so, go on to the next lesson. If you have more than eight incorrect frames, repeat the lesson until you reach the goal or until you have done the lesson five times, at which point you should go on to the next lesson regardless of the number of errors.

When you have done this series, take Test B13.

B13-1 Sightsinging

Sing each frame in time with the metronome and compare your response with the melody you then hear. The starting tone is given for the first frame only. Tally errors on a separate sheet of paper. Goal: No more than eight incorrect frames.

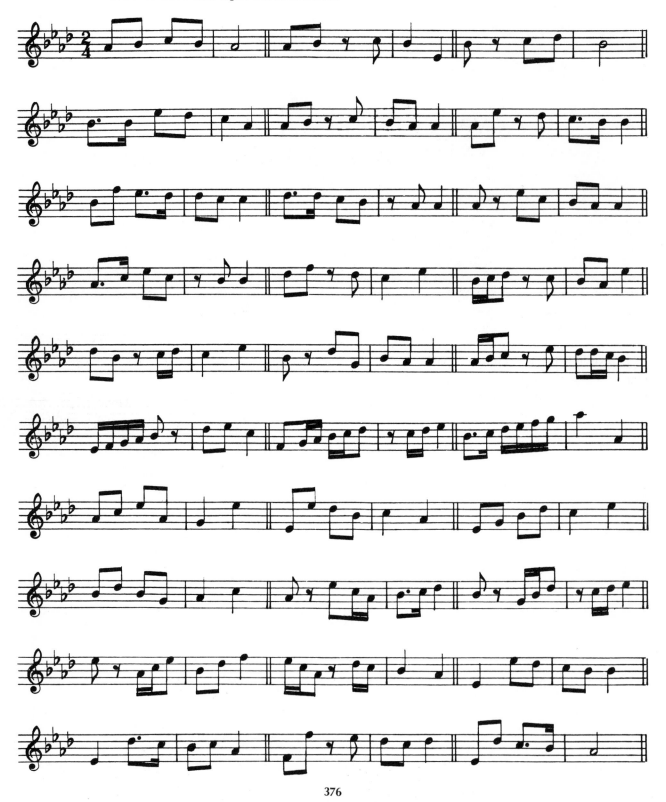

377

B13-2 Sightsinging

Sing each frame in time with the metronome and compare your response with the melody you then hear. The starting tone is given for the first frame only. Tally errors on a separate sheet of paper. Goal: No more than eight incorrect frames.

379

B13-3 Sightsinging

Sing each frame in time with the metronome and compare your response with the melody you then hear. The starting tone is given for the first frame only. Tally errors on a separate sheet of paper. Goal: No more than eight incorrect frames.

381

B13-4 Sightsinging

Sing each frame in time with the metronome and compare your response with the melody you then hear. The starting tone is given for the first frame only. Tally errors on a separate sheet of paper. Goal: No more than eight incorrect frames.

382

B13-5 Sightsinging

Sing each frame in time with the metronome and compare your response with the melody you then hear. The starting tone is given for the first frame only. Tally errors on a separate sheet of paper. Goal: No more than eight incorrect frames.

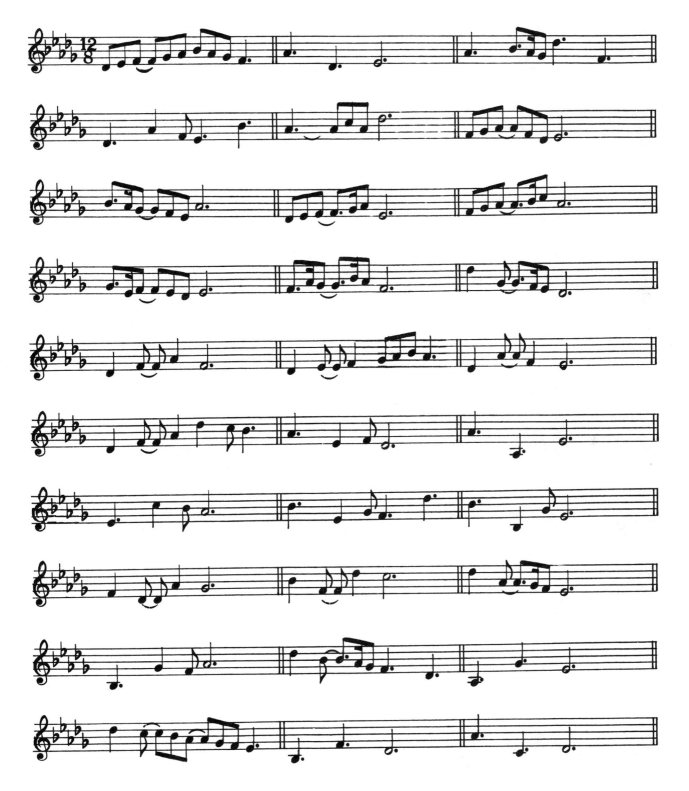

B13-6 Sightsinging

Sing each frame in time with the metronome and compare your response with the melody you then hear. The starting tone is given for the first frame only. Tally errors on a separate sheet of paper. Goal: No more than eight incorrect frames.

387

B13-7 Sightsinging

Sing each frame in time with the metronome and compare your response with the melody you then hear. The starting tone is given for the first frame only. Tally errors on a separate sheet of paper. Goal: No more than eight incorrect frames.

389

B13-8 Sightsinging

Sing each frame in time with the metronome and compare your response with the melody you then hear. The starting tone is given for the first frame only. Tally errors on a separate sheet of paper. Goal: No more than eight incorrect frames.

391

B13-9 Sightsinging

Sing each frame in time with the metronome and compare your response with the melody you then hear. The starting tone is given for the first frame only. Tally errors on a separate sheet of paper. Goal: No more than eight incorrect frames. After you have done this lesson, take Test B13.

393

Advanced Dictation— Melody and Rhythm SERIES B14

In this series there are six *melodic dictation lessons.* The procedure for the lessons in this series is the same as for Series B3: a printed worksheet and a tape recording are provided for each lesson. To do each frame, start by shielding the printed answer. When you have heard the melody, stop the tape and write the notes for the melody. Then slide the shield to the right and compare your response with the printed answer. Circle each frame in which your response is incorrect. Your goal is to complete each lesson with no more than eight incorrect frames. When you have done so, go on to the next lesson. If you have more than eight incorrect frames, repeat the lesson until you reach the goal or until you have done the lesson five times, at which point you should go on to the next lesson regardless of the number of errors.

When you have done this series, take Test B14.

B14-1 Melodic dictation
(Copy 1)

Shield the answer. Listen to the melody and notate it; then check your response. Circle incorrect responses. Stop the tape between frames. Goal: No more than eight incorrect frames.

396

B14-1 Melodic dictation

(Copy 2)

Shield the answer. Listen to the melody and notate it; then check your response. Circle incorrect responses. Stop the tape between frames. Goal: No more than eight incorrect frames.

399

B14-1 Melodic dictation
(Copy 3)

Shield the answer. Listen to the melody and notate it; then check your response. Circle incorrect responses. Stop the tape between frames. Goal: No more than eight incorrect frames.

402

404

B14-1 Melodic dictation
(Copy 4)

Shield the answer. Listen to the melody and notate it; then check your response. Circle incorrect responses. Stop the tape between frames. Goal: No more than eight incorrect frames.

405

407

B14-1 Melodic dictation

(Copy 5)

Shield the answer. Listen to the melody and notate it; then check your response. Circle incorrect responses. Stop the tape between frames. Goal: No more than eight incorrect frames.

409

B14-2 Melodic dictation

(Copy 1)

Shield the answer. Listen to the melody and notate it; then check your response. Circle incorrect responses. Stop the tape between frames. Goal: No more than eight incorrect frames.

413

B14-2 Melodic dictation
(Copy 2)

Shield the answer. Listen to the melody and notate it; then check your response. Circle incorrect responses. Stop the tape between frames. Goal: No more than eight incorrect frames.

416

B14-2 Melodic dictation

(Copy 3)

Shield the answer. Listen to the melody and notate it; then check your response. Circle incorrect responses. Stop the tape between frames. Goal: No more than eight incorrect frames.

417

419

B14-2 Melodic dictation

(Copy 4)

Shield the answer. Listen to the melody and notate it; then check your response. Circle incorrect responses. Stop the tape between frames. Goal: No more than eight incorrect frames.

421

422

B14-2 Melodic dictation
(Copy 5)

Shield the answer. Listen to the melody and notate it; then check your response. Circle incorrect responses. Stop the tape between frames. Goal: No more than eight incorrect frames.

423

424

B14-3 Melodic dictation
(Copy 1)

Shield the answer. Listen to the melody and notate it; then check your response. Circle incorrect responses. Stop the tape between frames. Goal: No more than eight incorrect frames.

426

427

428

B14-3 Melodic dictation

(Copy 2)

Shield the answer. Listen to the melody and notate it; then check your response. Circle incorrect responses. Stop the tape between frames. Goal: No more than eight incorrect frames.

429

430

431

B14-3 Melodic dictation
(Copy 3)

Shield the answer. Listen to the melody and notate it; then check your response. Circle incorrect responses. Stop the tape between frames. Goal: No more than eight incorrect frames.

432

433

434

B14-3 Melodic dictation

(Copy 4)

Shield the answer. Listen to the melody and notate it; then check your response. Circle incorrect responses. Stop the tape between frames. Goal: No more than eight incorrect frames.

436

437

B14-3 Melodic dictation

(Copy 5)

Shield the answer. Listen to the melody and notate it; then check your response. Circle incorrect responses. Stop the tape between frames. Goal: No more than eight incorrect frames.

440

B14-4 Melodic dictation

(Copy 1)

Shield the answer. Listen to the melody and notate it; then check your response. Circle incorrect responses. Stop the tape between frames. Goal: No more than eight incorrect frames.

441

442

443

B14-4 Melodic dictation

(Copy 2)

Shield the answer. Listen to the melody and notate it; then check your response. Circle incorrect responses. Stop the tape between frames. Goal: No more than eight incorrect frames.

445

B14-4 Melodic dictation

(Copy 3)

Shield the answer. Listen to the melody and notate it; then check your response. Circle incorrect responses. Stop the tape between frames. Goal: No more than eight incorrect frames.

447

448

449

B14-4 Melodic dictation

(Copy 4)

Shield the answer. Listen to the melody and notate it; then check your response. Circle incorrect responses. Stop the tape between frames. Goal: No more than eight incorrect frames.

450

451

452

B14-4 Melodic dictation
(Copy 5)

Shield the answer. Listen to the melody and notate it; then check your response. Circle incorrect responses. Stop the tape between frames. Goal: No more than eight incorrect frames.

453

454

B14-5 Melodic dictation
(Copy 1)

Shield the answer. Listen to the melody and notate it; then check your response. Circle incorrect responses. Stop the tape between frames. Goal: No more than eight incorrect frames.

456

457

B14-5 Melodic dictation

(Copy 2)

Shield the answer. Listen to the melody and notate it; then check your response. Circle incorrect responses. Stop the tape between frames. Goal: No more than eight incorrect frames.

459

460

461

B14-5 Melodic dictation
(Copy 3)

Shield the answer. Listen to the melody and notate it; then check your response. Circle incorrect responses. Stop the tape between frames. Goal: No more than eight incorrect frames.

462

463

B14-5 Melodic dictation
(Copy 4)

Shield the answer. Listen to the melody and notate it; then check your response. Circle incorrect responses. Stop the tape between frames. Goal: No more than eight incorrect frames.

465

466

467

B14-6 Melodic dictation
(Copy 1)

Shield the answer. Listen to the melody and notate it; then check your response. Circle incorrect responses. Stop the tape between frames. Goal: No more than eight incorrect frames. After you have done this lesson, take Test B14.

469

470

B14-6 Melodic dictation

(Copy 2)

Shield the answer. Listen to the melody and notate it; then check your response. Circle incorrect responses. Stop the tape between frames. Goal: No more than eight incorrect frames. After you have done this lesson, take Test B14.

473

B14-6 Melodic dictation

(Copy 3)

Shield the answer. Listen to the melody and notate it; then check your response. Circle incorrect responses. Stop the tape between frames. Goal: No more than eight incorrect frames. After you have done this lesson, take Test B14.

475

476

B14-6 Melodic dictation
(Copy 4)

Shield the answer. Listen to the melody and notate it; then check your response. Circle incorrect responses. Stop the tape between frames. Goal: No more than eight incorrect frames. After you have done this lesson, take Test B14.

477

478

479

Sightsinging–Complete Phrases with Modulations

In this series there are three lessons in *sightsinging complete phrases with modulations*. The purpose of these lessons is to develop your ability to sight-sing longer modulating melodies. A worksheet and a tape recording are provided for each lesson. Each frame on the worksheet takes a complete line. To do each frame, sing the complete melody with the tape stopped. Then start the tape and you will hear that portion of the melody which appears after the sign 𝄢. You should sing the entire melody, but judge the correctness of your response only on the part following the sign. You will hear the starting note for the first frame only. For all other frames you must find the starting note yourself with reference to the preceding frame. Count one error for each frame which is not entirely correct. Your goal is to complete each lesson with no more than six incorrect frames. When you have done so, go on to the next lesson. If you have more than six incorrect frames, repeat the lesson until you reach the goal or until you have done the lesson five times, at which point you should go on to the next lesson regardless of the number of errors.

When you have done this series, take Test B15.

B15-1 Sightsinging modulating phrases

Stop the tape while singing; then start the tape and compare your response. The tape contains only the portion of the melody after the sign. The starting tone is given only for the first frame. Goal: No more than six incorrect frames.

482

B15-2 Sightsinging modulating phrases

Stop the tape while singing; then start the tape and compare your response. The tape contains only the portion of the melody after the sign. The starting tone is given only for the first frame. Goal: No more than six incorrect frames.

486

B15-3 Sightsinging modulating phrases

Stop the tape while singing; then start the tape and compare your response. The tape contains only the portion of the melody after the sign. The starting tone is given only for the first frame. Goal: No more than six incorrect frames.

488

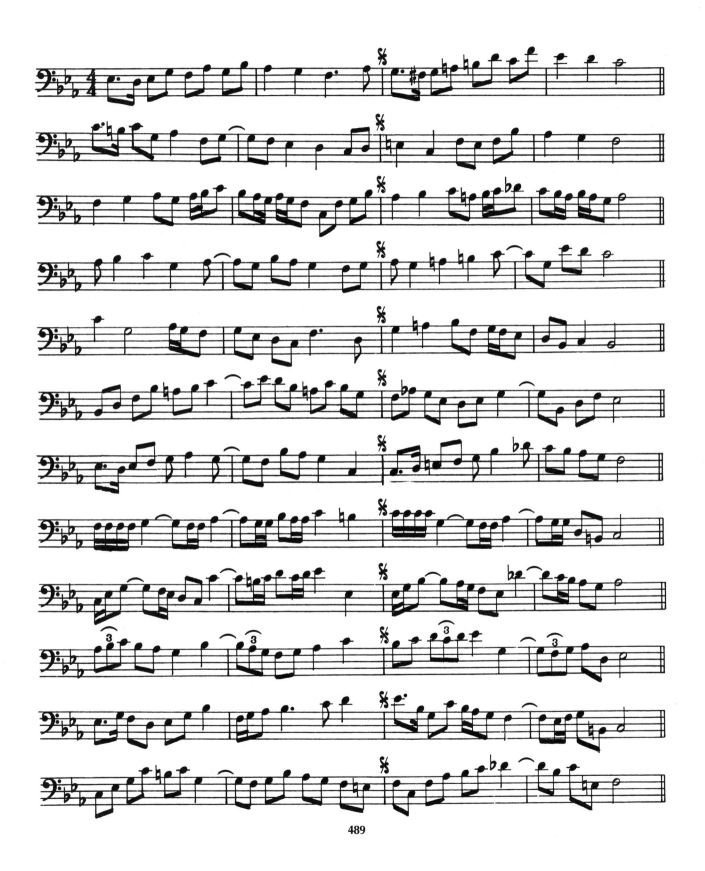

489

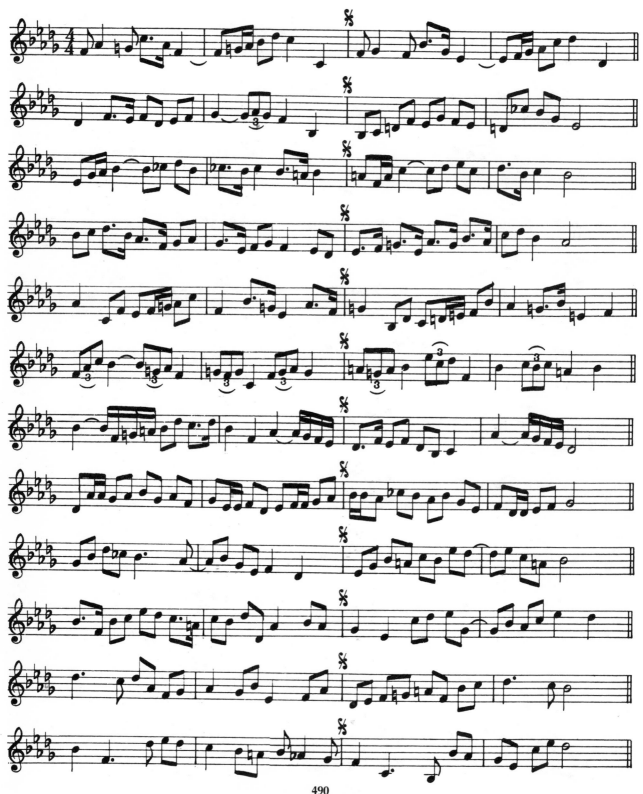

490

Dictation—Complete Phrases with Modulations

SERIES B16

In this series there are five lessons in *melodic dictation of complete phrases with modulations*. The procedure for these lessons is the same as for those in Series B8: a worksheet and a tape recording are provided for each lesson. Each frame on the worksheet takes a complete line. The clef and starting note for each melody appears at the beginning of the line. Write these on your own manuscript paper before listening to the melody. Then listen to the melody and write the key signature, time signature, bar lines, and notes. Use the signature of the key in which the melody begins and the appropriate accidentals where the modulations occur. Two time signatures are printed after the initial material. Choose the one for your response which is appropriate for the melody. Stop the tape at the conclusion of the melody. Each melody is recorded twice on the tape recording. You may rewind the tape if you desire additional hearings. On the test for this series, each melody will be heard four times, so you should attempt to complete each frame in no more than four hearings. When you have completed your response, compare it to the printed answer. Each lesson in this series should be done only once in preparation for the test. The test itself will serve to measure your achievement. If you wish to raise your test score, you should do each of the lessons once more and then take the test again.

When you have done this series, take Test B16.

B16-1 Melodic dictation of complete phrases

Write the initial material on your own manuscript paper. The melody appears twice on the tape. Rewind the tape for additional hearings. Write the key signature (in which the melody begins), time signature, bar lines, and notes; then check your response. Do this lesson once in preparation for the test.

492

B16-2 Melodic dictation of complete phrases

Write the initial material on your own manuscript paper. The melody appears twice on the tape.
Rewind the tape for additional hearings. Write the key signature (in which the melody begins), time
signature, bar lines, and notes; then check your response. Do this lesson once in preparation for
the test.

493

B16-3 Melodic dictation of complete phrases

Write the initial material on your own manuscript paper. The melody appears twice on the tape. Rewind the tape for additional hearings. Write the key signature (in which the melody begins), time signature, bar lines, and notes; then check your response. Do this lesson once in preparation for the test.

494

B16-4 Melodic dictation of complete phrases

Write the initial material on your own manuscript paper. The melody appears twice on the tape. Rewind the tape for additional hearings. Write the key signature (in which the melody begins), time signature, bar lines, and notes; then check your response. Do this lesson once in preparation for the test.

B16-5 Melodic dictation of complete phrases

Write the initial material on your own manuscript paper. The melody appears twice on the tape. Rewind the tape for additional hearings. Write the key signature (in which the melody begins), time signature, bar lines, and notes; then check your response. Do this lesson once in preparation for the test. After you have done this lesson, take Test B16.

496

Advanced Sightsinging— Complete Phrases

In this series, there are three lessons in *sightsinging complete phrases*. The procedure for these lessons is the same as for those in Series B6: a worksheet and a tape recording are provided for each lesson. Each frame on the worksheet takes a complete line. To do each frame, start by listening to the tape. You will hear a metronome clicking at the tempo in which you should sing and you will be given the pitch of the first note of the frame. Observe the metronome marking on the worksheet to determine what note value receives one beat of the metronome. After hearing the initial material, stop the tape and sing the melody. Then starting the tape, you will hear a correct performance of the melody and can judge if your response was correct. Each lesson in this series should be done only once in preparation for the test. The test itself will serve to measure your achievement. If you wish to raise your test score, you should do each lesson once more and then take the test again.

When you have done this series, take Test B17.

B17-1 Sightsinging complete phrases

Listen to starting tone and metronome. Stop the tape and sing the phrase. Then start the tape and compare your response. Do this lesson once in preparation for the test.

B17-2 Sightsinging complete phrases

Listen to starting tone and metronome. Stop the tape and sing the phrase. Then start the tape and compare your response. Do this lesson once in preparation for the test.

B17-3 Sightsinging complete phrases

Listen to starting tone and metronome. Stop the tape and sing the phrase. Then start the tape and compare your response. Do this lesson once in preparation for the test. After you have done this lesson, take Test B17.

503

Test Record Sheet

TEST	MAXIMUM	LEVEL			SCORE AND DATE
		1	2	3	
B1	300	244	200	155	
B2	350	291	233	175	
B3	300	244	200	155	
B4	300	244	200	155	
B5	400	333	266	200	
B6	400	325	266	207	
B7	400	320	260	200	
B8	300	262	225	187	
B9	400	314	257	200	
B10	300	250	200	150	
B11	300	244	200	155	
B12	350	280	227	175	
B13	400	333	266	200	
B14	400	325	266	207	
B15	500	416	333	250	
B16	500	314	257	200	
B17	500	400	325	250	

All test scores are weighted to compensate for the varying length, difficulty, and importance of the series. The maximum score is the highest attainable score on a test. Level 1 represents high achievement. Level 2 represents moderate or average achievement. Level 3 represents low but significant achievement.

A 0
B 1
C 2
D 3
E 4
F 5
G 6
H 7
I 8
J 9